A+ LAB MANUAL

FOR MANAGING AND MAINTAINING YOUR PC

THIRD EDITION

CLINT SAXTON, MCSE, MCT, A+

ONE MAIN STREET, CAMBRIDGE, MA 02142

Australia • Canada • Denmark • Japan • Mexico • New Zealand • Philippines
Puerto Rico • Singapore • South Africa • Spain • United Kingdom • United States

A+ Lab Manual for Guide to Managing and Maintaining Your PC, Third Edition, is published by Course Technology.

Associate Publisher:	Kristen Duerr
Product Manager:	Lisa Ayers Egan
Production Editor:	Jennifer Goguen
Developmental Editor:	Lisa Ruffolo, The Software Resource
Quality Assurance:	John Bosco
Editorial Assistant:	Jennifer Adams
Composition House:	GEX Publishing Services
Text Designer:	GEX Publishing Services
Cover Designer:	John Gomes
Marketing Manager:	Susan Ogar

Trademarks

Course Technology and A+ are registered trademarks.

Disclaimer

Course Technology reserves the right to revise this publication and make changes from time to time in its content without notice.

The Web addresses in this book are subject to change from time to time as necessary without notice.

For more information, contact Course Technology, One Main Street, Cambridge, MA 02142; or find us on the World Wide Web at *www.course.com*.

For permission to use material from this text or product, contact us by

- Web: www.thomsonrights.com
- Phone: 1-800-730-2214
- Fax: 1-800-730-2215

ISBN 0-619-01536-5

Printed in America

2 3 4 5 6 7 8 9 BM 02 01 00 99

TABLE OF CONTENTS

CHAPTER 16

CHAPTER 17

CHAPTER 18

CHAPTER 19

PREFACE

Use this Lab Manual as a dynamic tool to gain direct experience setting up and repairing personal computers. Designed to be used in conjunction with the Third Edition of the *A+ Guide to Managing and Maintaining Your PC* by Jean Andrews, this manual merges tutorial and lab experiences for complete understanding of PC maintenance and thorough preparation for the A+ service technician exams. Inside this manual you will discover 67 exciting labs tailored to provide simulated real–life experience through hands–on exercises. At the end of each lab exercise, a Certification Objectives section clearly outlines the A+ skills you have mastered. After completing all 67 lab exercises, you will have not only practiced each A+ objective in a hands–on environment, but will have also gained valuable Windows NT installation and configuration skills, which are vital in the quickly evolving PC industry.

This edition of the *A+ Lab Manual* now includes a new chapter on laser printers, new labs on installing and configuring CD-ROM drives and Windows 98, and updated review questions to test the new material. It also covers Microsoft Windows ® NT and Windows 98, and is current for today's technology.

This book provides comprehensive preparation for the revised A+ Certification examinations offered through the Computer Technology Industry Association (CompTIA). Because the popularity of this certification credential is quickly growing among employers, obtaining certification increases your ability to gain employment, improve your salary, and enhance your career. To find more information about A+ Certification and its sponsoring organization, CompTIA, see their Web site at *www.comptia.org.*

Uniquely designed with you in mind, this workbook is written from the "show-me" perspective—instead of simply describing a procedure or task, this manual shows you how to complete it, step by step. Each lab lets you interact with a PC, gives you the freedom to make mistakes, and most importantly, enables you to recover and LEARN from those mistakes in a safe environment. If your goal is to become an A+ certified technician, develop an understanding of operating systems, or become a PC hardware technician, the *A+ Lab Manual*, along with the *A+ Managing and Maintaining Your PC* textbook, will take you there!

Features

In order to ensure a successful experience for both instructors and students, this book includes the following pedagogical features:

- **Objectives**—Every lab opens with a list of learning objectives that sets the stage for students to absorb the lessons of the lab.

- **Materials Required**—This feature outlines all the materials students need to complete the lab successfully.

- **Lab Setup & Safety Tips**—This quick list summarizes any safety precautions or preliminary steps instructors and students should take before beginning a lab.

- **Activity**—Every lab activity is broken down into manageable sections to ensure the student understands each step of the lab.

- **Lab Notes**—These notes provide the key definitions and acronyms used in the body of the lab.

- **Certification Objectives**—These tables illustrate the A+ objectives reinforced by each lab.

- **Review Questions**—Exercises at the end of each lab let students test their understanding of the lab material.

- **Web Site**—For updates to this book and information about other PC Repair products available, go to *www.course.com/pcrepair*

Acknowledgments

I would like to give a special thanks to Jamie and Derek Olds as well as George Marroquin for their contributions and support throughout this entire project. I would also like give a warm and special thanks to my significant other, Laura Shelton, for her patience and support throughout this project and others. Thank you all for your encouragement, patience, and support.

I would like to extend my sincere appreciation to Lisa Ruffolo, Lisa Egan, and the other Course Technology managers and editors for their instrumental roles in the creation and design of this Lab Manual.

Many thanks also to the reviewers for their insights and valuable input. A sincere thank you to:

A. Peter Anderson   Blackhawk Technical Institute
Larry Bohn   Stream International Training
Mike Canzano   Toronto School of Business

PROTECT YOURSELF, YOUR HARDWARE, AND YOUR SOFTWARE

When you work on a computer it is possible to harm both the computer and yourself. The most common accident that happens when attempting to fix a computer problem is the erasing of software or data. Experimenting without knowing what you are doing can cause damage. To prevent these sorts of accidents, as well as the physically dangerous ones, take a few safety precautions. The text below describes the potential sources of damage to computers and how to protect against them.

Power to the Computer

To protect both yourself and the equipment when working inside a computer, turn off the power, unplug the computer, and always use a grounding bracelet. Consider the monitor and the power supply to be "black boxes." Never remove the cover or put your hands inside this equipment unless you know about the hazards of charged capacitors. Both the power supply and the monitor can hold a dangerous level of electricity even after they are turned off and disconnected from a power source.

Static Electricity, or ESD

Electrostatic discharge (ESD), commonly known as static electricity, is an electrical charge at rest. A static charge can build up on the surface of a nongrounded conductor and on nonconductive surfaces such as clothing or plastic. When two objects with dissimilar electrical charges touch, static electricity passes between them until the dissimilar charges are made equal. To see how this works, turn off the lights in a room, scuff your feet on the carpet, and touch another person. Occasionally you may see and feel the charge in your fingers. If you can feel the charge, then you discharged at least 3,000 volts of static electricity. If you hear the discharge, then you released at least 6,000 volts. If you see the discharge, then you released at least 8,000 volts of ESD. A charge of less than 3,000 volts can damage most electronic components. You can touch a chip on an expansion card or system board and damage the chip with ESD and never feel, hear, or see the discharge.

There are two types of damage that ESD can cause in an electronic component: catastrophic failures and upset failures. A catastrophic failure destroys the component beyond use. An upset failure damages the component so that it does not perform well, even though it may still function to some degree. Upset failures are the most difficult to detect because they are not easily observed.

Protect Against ESD

To protect the computer against ESD, always ground yourself before touching electronic components, including the hard drive, system board, expansion cards, processors, and memory modules. Ground yourself and the computer parts, using one or more of the following static control devices or methods:

- *Ground bracelet or static strap:* A ground bracelet is a strap you wear around your wrist. The other end is attached to a grounded conductor such as the computer case or a ground mat, or it can plug into a wall outlet (only the ground prong makes a connection!).

- *Rubber mats or ground mats:* Ground mats can come equipped with a cord to plug into a wall outlet to provide a grounded surface on which to work. Remember, if you lift the component off the mat, it is no longer grounded and is susceptible to ESD.

- *Static shielding bags:* New components come shipped in static shielding bags. Save the bags to store other devices that are not currently installed in a PC.

The best solution to protect against ESD is to use a ground bracelet together with a ground mat. Consider a ground bracelet to be essential equipment when working on a computer. However, if you find yourself in a situation where you must work without one, touch the computer case before you touch a component. When passing a chip to another person, ground yourself. Leave components inside their protective bags until ready to use. Work on hard floors, not carpet, or use antistatic spray on the carpets. Generally, don't work on a computer if you or the computer have just come inside from the cold.

Besides using a grounding mat, you can also create a ground for the computer case by leaving the power cord to the case plugged into the wall outlet. This is safe enough because the power is turned off when you work inside the case. However, if you happen to touch an exposed area of the power switch inside the case, it is possible to get a shock. Because of this risk, in this book, you are directed to unplug the power cord to the PC before you work inside the case.

There is an exception to the ground-yourself rule. Inside a monitor case, the electricity stored in capacitors poses a substantial danger. When working inside a monitor, you *don't* want to be grounded, as you would provide a conduit for the voltage to discharge through your body. In this situation, be careful *not* to ground yourself.

When handling system boards and expansion cards, don't touch the chips on the boards. Don't stack boards on top of each other, which could accidentally dislodge a chip. Hold cards by the edges, but don't touch the edge connections on the card.

Don't touch a chip with a magnetized screwdriver. When using a multimeter to measure electricity, be careful not to touch a chip with the probes. When changing DIP switches, don't use a graphite pencil, because graphite is magnetized; a ballpoint pen works very well.

After you unpack a new device or software that has been wrapped in cellophane, remove the cellophane from the work area quickly. Don't allow anyone who is not properly grounded to touch components. Do not store expansion cards within one foot of a monitor, because the monitor can discharge as much as 29,000 volts of ESD onto the screen.

Hold an expansion card by the edges. Don't touch any of the soldered components on a card. If you need to put an electronic device down, place it on a grounded mat or on a static shielding bag. Keep components away from your hair and clothing.

Protect Hard Drives and Disks

Always turn off a computer before moving it to protect the hard drive, which is always spinning when the computer is turned on (unless the drive has a sleep mode). Never jar a computer while the hard disk is running. Avoid placing a PC on the floor, where the user can accidentally kick it.

Follow the usual precautions to protect disks. Keep them away from magnetic fields, heat, and extreme cold. Don't open the floppy shuttle window or touch the surface of the disk inside the housing. Treat disks with care and they'll generally last for years.

CHAPTER 1

HOW COMPUTERS WORK—AN OVERVIEW

LABS INCLUDED IN THIS CHAPTER

♦ LAB 1.1   COMPONENTS OF A PERSONAL COMPUTER SYSTEM

♦ LAB 1.2   OPERATING A DOS-BASED PC

♦ LAB 1.3   OPERATING A WINDOWS 3.x-BASED PC

♦ LAB 1.4   OPERATING A WINDOWS 95/98-BASED PC

LAB 1.1 COMPONENTS OF A PERSONAL COMPUTER SYSTEM

Objective

The objective of this lab is to introduce you to the components of a personal computer (PC) system, which include: monitor, keyboard, mouse, printer, printer cable, power cables, and system unit. After completing this lab exercise you will be able to:

- Identify the various components of a PC system.
- Describe the functionality of the various PC system components.
- Attach each of the most commonly used devices.
- Properly perform basic cleaning and maintenance procedures for each of the most commonly used PC components.

Materials Required

This lab will require one complete lab workstation for every four students. The lab workstations should meet the following requirements:

- 486 processor
- At least 4MB of RAM
- 540MB or larger hard drive

Labels for each group of students

Paper towels for each group of students

At least two spray bottles filled with a cleaning solution of either water and ammonia or water and liquid soap

One demonstration PC with each of the following components properly attached and labeled:

- Monitor
- Keyboard
- Mouse
- Printer
- Printer cable
- Power cables
- System unit

Lab Setup & Safety Tips

Each group of students should have all of the following PC components unattached:

- Monitor
- Keyboard
- Mouse
- Power cables
- System unit

ACTIVITY

Attaching your lab workstation's devices

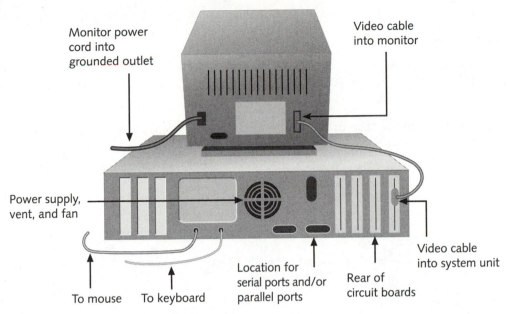

Monitor power cord into grounded outlet

Video cable into monitor

Power supply, vent, and fan

To mouse   To keyboard

Location for serial ports and/or parallel ports

Rear of circuit boards

Video cable into system unit

Figure 1-1   Cables connected to ports

1. Observe the configuration of your instructor's demonstration PC.

2. Write down the name and function of each device labeled on your instructor's demonstration PC.

3. Attach your lab workstation's components in the same manner as on your instructor's demonstration PC.

4. Power on your lab workstation to verify that each component has been properly connected.

5. After your instructor has verified proper operation, power down your system.

Cleaning your mouse

1. Turn the mouse upside down.

2. Locate and remove the cover of the mouse ball.

3. Remove the mouse ball.

4. Inside the housing of the mouse ball, you will find several rollers. Clear these rollers of debris.

5. After clearing any debris from the rollers, replace the mouse ball and cover.

Cleaning your monitor

1. Lightly spray a paper towel with water or a manufacturer-recommended cleaning solution from a spray bottle (never spray anything directly on the screen of your monitor).

2. Gently wipe the entire screen using the slightly damp paper towel.

Clearing a stuck key

Most keyboards are designed to allow you to remove the keys by gently pulling or prying the key upward. This procedure is most commonly used when debris has become jammed underneath a particular key.

Cleaning the exterior case of the system unit

1. Lightly spray a paper towel with water or a manufacturer-recommended cleaning solution from a spray bottle (never spray anything directly on the exterior of your system unit case).

2. Gently wipe the entire case using the slightly damp paper towel.

Lab Notes

Although every PC has different peripherals and types of devices, all PCs require several components, which are listed below:

- Monitor

- Keyboard

- Mouse

- Power cables

- System unit

 ## CERTIFICATION OBJECTIVES

Table 1-1   Core A+ Objectives

Objectives	Chapters	Page Numbers
1.1 Identify basic terms, concepts, and functions of system modules, including how each module should work during normal operation.	1, 2, 11, 15	
1.2 Identify basic procedures for adding and removing field replaceable modules.	1, 3, 4, 11, 14	
F. Input devices	1, 14	5, 14, 780-782
3.1 Identify the purpose of various types of preventive maintenance products and procedures and when to use/perform them.	17, 18	
A. Liquid cleaning compounds	18	
B. Types of materials to clean contacts and connections	17, 18	941, 978, 979

Review Questions

Circle True or False.

1. A monitor requires one cord and one cable to function properly.   True / False

2. Most keyboards have their own power source.   True / False

3. The mouse and keyboard connections are interchangeable.   True / False

4. How many cables and cords are connected to the system unit, and to which devices are they connected?

_____

_____

_____

_____

_____

5. You are employed as a desktop PC support technician at the PC Store. Matt, one of your customers, has called you with a problem. He explains that he just finished moving his PC and reconnecting all of the cables, but now he is getting error messages and both the keyboard and mouse won't work. What is the most likely cause of Matt's problem?

_____

_____

_____

_____

_____

6. Another customer, Judy, also has just finished moving her PC, but now the monitor screen is blank. She explains that the power light for the monitor is turned on and that the system unit power light is also on. Which cables would you ask Judy to check first?

_____

_____

_____

_____

_____

7. Describe how to clean a mouse.

_____

_____

_____

_____

_____

LAB 1.2 OPERATING A DOS-BASED PC

Objective

The objective of this lab exercise is to provide you with the experience of creating both files and directories in the DOS environment. After completing this lab exercise you will be able to:

- Start a DOS computer.
- Start a DOS application.
- Create a DOS system disk.
- Create a directory.
- Create and save a text file.
- Describe the purpose of a system disk.
- Properly shut down your DOS lab workstation.

Materials Required

One MS-DOS lab workstation is necessary for every three students. The lab workstations should meet the following requirements:

- 486 or better
- At least 4MB of RAM
- 540MB or larger hard drive

One unformatted floppy disk for each lab workstation

Lab Setup & Safety Tips

- This lab assumes that the DOS operating system is installed in a directory called DOS.
- Each lab workstation should have MS-DOS 5.0 or greater installed and functioning properly.
- After completing this lab exercise, be sure to keep your system disk in a safe place; you will use it in future labs.

ACTIVITY

Creating a DOS system disk

1. Power on your lab workstation, and allow it to boot into the DOS environment.
2. Place the blank floppy disk in drive A.
3. At the C prompt, type **FORMAT A:**.
4. Press **Enter** and respond to the formatting prompts.
5. After the disk has been formatted, type **SYS C: A:**.
6. Press **Enter**.
7. Type **CD DOS** and press **Enter**.
8. Type **COPY FDISK.EXE A:** and press **Enter**.
9. Type **COPY FORMAT.COM A:** and press **Enter**.
10. Type **COPY SCANDISK.EXE A:** and press **Enter**.
11. Type **COPY DEFRAG.EXE A:** and press **Enter**.

Understanding a DOS system disk

1. Place the system disk in drive A.

2. Turn on the PC.

3. Record the results. _____

4. Turn off the PC.

5. Place a blank disk in drive A.

6. Turn on the PC.

7. Record the results. _____

8. Turn off the PC.

9. Remove the floppy disk from drive A.

Creating a file using DOS EDIT

1. Turn on the PC, and allow it to boot into the DOS environment.

2. At the C prompt, type **EDIT** and then press **ESC**.

3. Type **This is a test file** in the Edit program.

4. Press **Alt + F** (hold down the Alt key and at the same time press the letter F).

5. Press the down arrow [↓] key to select **Save As** from the File menu.

6. At the top of the Save As dialog box, locate the **File Name** section.

7. Type **C:\Test.txt** as the filename.

8. Press **Enter**.

9. Press **Alt + F**.

10. Press the down arrow [↓] key to select **Exit** from the File menu.

Creating a directory

1. At the C prompt, type **MD C:\LAB1.2** and press **Enter**. Your lab workstation should respond by returning you to a C prompt.

2. Type **CD LAB1.2** and press **Enter**. Your lab workstation should respond with the following prompt: **C:\LAB.1.2>**. This means that you are now in the **LAB1.2** directory.

3. Change back to the root directory by typing **CD ..** . Your lab workstation should return to the C prompt (C:>) or root directory.

Lab Notes

EDIT—The Edit program is a DOS text editor that lets you create and modify text files in the DOS environment.

DOS system disk—A DOS system disk is a bootable disk that boots a PC using a minimal amount of DOS system files.

MD—The MD, or Make Directory command, is used to create a directory in the DOS environment.

How do I shut down DOS?—DOS is one of the simplest operating systems to shut down; you simply power off the PC.

A^+ | **CERTIFICATION OBJECTIVES**

Table 1-2   DOS/Windows A+ Objectives

Objectives	Chapters	Page Numbers
1.1 Identify the operating system's functions, structure, and major system files.	1, 2, 4, 12, Appendices C and E	
A. Functions of DOS, Windows 3.x and Windows 95.	1, 2	35, 74
1.2 Identify ways to navigate the operating system and how to get to needed technical information.	1, 12	
A. Procedures (e.g., menu or icon - driven) for navigating through DOS to perform such things as locating, accessing, and retrieving information.	1	44

Review Questions

Circle True or False.

1. When booting an MS-DOS computer, you must always have a system disk in drive A. True / False

2. Before powering off a DOS system, you should first execute the SHUTDOWN DOS command.   True / False

3. Only blank disks can be used as system disks.   True / False

4. You can use the Edit program to create DOS system disks.   True / False

5. Describe the most obvious difference between a DOS system disk and other formatted disks.

   _____

   _____

   _____

   _____

6. You are working as a PC desktop support technician at the Fun Job Corporation. Kyle, one of your customers, just rebooted his PC after copying some files from a disk to his hard drive. Kyle says that he is receiving the error message, "Non-system disk or disk error," and it keeps repeating that error no matter what he does. Describe what the problem is and how Kyle should resolve it.

   _____

   _____

   _____

   _____

LAB 1.3 OPERATING A WINDOWS 3.X-BASED PC

Objective

The objective of this lab exercise is to show you how to operate and navigate in the Windows 3.x environment. After completing this lab exercise, you will be able to:

- Start a Windows 3.x-based computer.
- Start an application on a Windows 3.x-based computer.
- Create and save a text file in the Windows 3.x environment.
- Create a directory using File Manager.
- Shut down your Windows 3.x lab workstation.

Materials Required

One Windows 3.x lab workstation is needed for every three students. The lab workstation should meet the following requirements:

- 486 or better
- At least 4MB of RAM
- 540MB or larger hard drive

Lab Setup & Safety Tips

- Each lab workstation should have Window 3.x installed and functioning properly.

ACTIVITY

Creating a text file in Windows 3.x

1. Power on the lab workstation, and allow it to boot into the Windows environment.
2. In Program Manager, double-click the **Accessories** group icon.
3. Double-click the **Notepad** program icon.
4. In the Notepad window, type **This a test file**.
5. In the upper-left corner of the Notepad window, click the **File** menu, and then click **Save As**.
6. In the File Name section of the Save As dialog box, type **Test.txt**.
7. Click the **Save** button.
8. In the Notepad window, click **File**, and then click **Exit**.
9. Click the **Close** button to close the Accessories window.

Creating a directory

1. Locate the Main group in the **Program Manager** window.
2. Double-click **Main**.
3. Double-click **File Manager**.
4. Click your **drive C** icon to highlight it.
5. In the upper-left corner of the File Manager window, click the **File** menu.
6. Click **Create Directory**.

7. Type **LAB1.3** and press **Enter**.

8. Verify that the directory was created by looking on your drive C for a yellow folder called LAB1.3.

9. In the File Manager window, click **file** on the menu bar, and then click **Exit**.

10. In the main window, click **file** on the menu bar, and then click **Exit**.

Shutting down Windows 3.x

1. In the Program Manager window, click the **File** menu, and then click **Exit Windows**.

2. Click the **Yes** button when prompted.

3. When Windows has exited to DOS, power off the lab workstation.

 Lab Notes

Notepad—Notepad is the Windows 3.x equivalent of the DOS Edit program. It is a simple text editor you can use to create and modify text files.

File Manager—File Manager is a Windows-based utility designed to simplify file and directory management.

 ## CERTIFICATION OBJECTIVES

Table 1-3   DOS/Windows A+ Objectives

Objectives	Chapters	Page Numbers
1.1 Identify the operating system's functions, structure, and major system files.	1, 2, 4, 12, Appendices C and E	
A. Functions of DOS, Windows 3.x and Windows 95.	1, 2	35, 74
1.2 Identify ways to navigate the operating system and how to get to needed technical information.	1, 12	
A. Procedures (e.g., menu or icon - driven) for navigating through DOS to perform such things as locating, accessing, and retrieving information.	1	44
B. Procedures for navigating through the Windows 3.x/Windows 95/98 operating system, accessing, and retrieving information.	1, 12	49, 50, 600, 601

Review Questions

Circle True or False.

1. You can use either Windows or DOS to create a directory.   True / False

2. To create a directory in Windows 3.x, you can use the Notepad program.   True / False

3. Notepad is the equivalent of the DOS command MD.   True / False

4. Where is the Notepad icon found by default in Windows 3.x?

_____

_____

_____

_____

5. Rick is trying to find an important document that he misplaced. He wants to locate the document using File Manager, but can't remember how to start it. List the instructions you would give Rick to help him start File Manager.

_____

_____

_____

_____

_____

6. Tom has written a quick letter in Notepad. He now wants to save the letter to drive C. Describe how Tom should save his letter from within Notepad.

_____

_____

_____

_____

_____

LAB 1.4 OPERATING A WINDOWS 95/98-BASED PC

Objective

The objective of this lab exercise is to show you how to operate and navigate in the Windows 95/98 environment. After completing this lab exercise, you will be able to:

- Start a Windows 95 or Windows 98 computer.
- Start an application within Windows 95 or Windows 98.
- Create and save a text file in the Windows 95/98 environment.
- Create a directory using Windows Explorer.
- Properly shut down a Windows 95 or 98 computer.

Materials Required

One Windows 95 and one Windows 98 lab workstation for every six students. The lab workstations should meet the following requirements:

- 486 or better
- At least 16MB of RAM
- 540MB or larger hard drive
- Windows 95/98

Lab Setup & Safety Tips

- The classroom workstations should be divided; half should have Windows 95 and the other half should have Windows 98. Students should work in groups so that each has access to both a Windows 95 and a Windows 98 computer.

ACTIVITY

Creating a text file in Windows 95 and Windows 98

1. Power on the lab workstation and allow it to boot into the Windows environment.
2. Click the **Start** button.
3. Point to **Programs**, and then point to **Accessories**.
4. Click **Notepad**.
5. In the Notepad window, type **This is a test file**.
6. In the upper-left corner of the Notepad window, click the **File** menu, and then click **Save As**.
7. In the File Name section of the Save As dialog box, type **Test.txt**.
8. Click the **Save** button.
9. In the Notepad window, click **File**, and then click **Exit**.

Creating a folder (directory) in the Windows 95/98 environment

1. Click the **Start** button.
2. Point to **Programs**.
3. Click **Windows Explorer**.
4. Click your **drive C** icon to highlight it.

5. In the upper-left corner of the Windows Explorer, click the **File** menu.

6. Point to **New** and click **Folder**.

7. Type **LAB1.4** and press **Enter**.

8. Verify that the directory was created by looking on your drive C for a yellow folder called LAB1.4.

Shutting down Windows 95/98

1. Click the **Start** button.

2. Click **Shut Down**.

3. Select the **Shut Down the computer?** option in the Shut Down Windows dialog box, and then click the **Yes** button.

4. Wait for Windows to completely shut down and tell you that it is safe to turn off your computer.

Lab Notes

Notepad—Notepad is the Windows 95/98 equivalent of the DOS Edit program. It is simply a text editor you can use to create and modify text files.

Windows Explorer—The Windows Explorer is a Windows-based utility designed to simplify file and directory management. It is the Windows 95/98 equivalent of File Manager.

What is the difference between a folder and a directory?—A folder and a directory are the same thing. The difference lies in the operating system you are using. In the DOS environment, the correct term is directory, whereas in the Windows 95/98 environment, the term is folder.

What is the difference between Windows 95 and Windows 98?—Windows 98 includes FAT32 support, updated drivers, enhanced security features, and USB support, whereas Windows 95 does not include these features.

CERTIFICATION OBJECTIVES

Table 1-4   DOS/Windows A+ Objectives

Objectives	Chapters	Page Numbers
1.1 Identify the operating system's functions, structure, and major system files.	1, 2, 4, 12, Appendices C and E	
A. Functions of DOS, Windows 3.x and Windows 95/98.	1, 2	35, 74
C. Contrasts between Windows 3.x and Windows 95/98.	1, 12	36, 624-630
1.2 Identify ways to navigate the operating system and how to get to needed technical information.	1, 2	
A. Procedures (e.g., menu or icon - driven) for navigating through DOS to perform such things as locating, accessing, and retrieving information.	1	44
B. Procedures for navigating through the Windows 3.x and Windows 95/98 operating systems, accessing, and retrieving information.	1, 12	49, 50, 600, 601

Review Questions

Circle True or False.

1. The Notepad program in Windows 95/98 is included in the Accessories group.
True / False

2. You can use Notepad to write short text files.   True / False

3. Using Notepad you can create and manipulate only one text document at a time.
True / False

4. Where can you find the Accessories group in the Windows 95/98 environment?

_____

_____

_____

_____

_____

5. Windows Explorer is a replacement for the Windows 3.x _____ utility.

6. You are employed at the Happy Day Corporation. Bill, the manager of your department, has a laptop with Windows 95. He is new to the Windows 95 environment and is trying to shut down his computer. List the instructions you would give Bill to properly shut down his Windows 95 laptop.

_____

_____

_____

_____

_____

How Software and Hardware Work Together

LABS INCLUDED IN THIS CHAPTER

♦ **Lab 2.1** **CMOS Manipulation**

♦ **Lab 2.2** **IRQ and DMA Management**

♦ **Lab 2.3** **I/O Management**

♦ **Lab 2.4** **The Boot Process**

Lab 2.1 CMOS Manipulation

Objective

The objective of this lab is to familiarize you with the operation of your lab workstation's Complementary Metal–Oxide Semiconductor (CMOS) Setup program. After completing this lab exercise, you will be able to:

- Use the CMOS Setup program to customize the operation and configuration of a PC.

Materials Required

One Windows 9x lab workstation for every four students. The lab workstations should meet the following requirements:

- 486 or better
- At least 16MB of RAM
- 540MB or larger hard drive

Lab Setup & Safety Tips

- Because there are so many different types of setup programs, it is recommended that you ask for some basic tips from your instructor before proceeding.

Activity

Creating a System Configuration Worksheet

A System Configuration Worksheet is a spreadsheet or other type of document that contains all of your workstation's CMOS configuration parameters. Use the sections below to develop your own System Configuration Worksheet for your lab workstation.

For each of the following system components, record the information currently saved in your lab workstation's CMOS:

CPU _____

Memory _____

IDE 1 _____

IDE 2 _____

IDE 3 _____

IDE 4 _____

SCSI _____

Serial 1 _____

Serial 2 _____

LPT 1 _____

Network card _____

CACHE _____

2

Changing CMOS values

1. Review the System Configuration Worksheet provided for your computer.

2. Start your PC.

3. Following the instructions provided on your screen, enter the Setup program.

4. Change the DATE for your computer to **today's date**, in the year 2000.

5. Change the Hard Disk Drive configuration to **NONE**.

6. Save your changes.

7. Shut down your computer, and allow it to reboot.

8. Observe the changes in the startup sequence.

9. Enter the Setup program.

10. Reconfigure your hard drive to match the parameters of your System Configuration Worksheet.

11. Activate the Power Management on your PC.

12. Assign the password of **LAB** in all uppercase letters to your system Setup program.

13. Save your changes.

14. Shut down your computer and allow it to reboot.

15. Observe the changes in the startup sequence.

Restoring your lab workstation using the System Configuration Worksheet

1. Type the system startup password.

2. Enter the Setup program.

3. Disable the system startup password.

4. Referring to the System Configuration Worksheet, verify that all CMOS settings have returned to their original configuration.

Lab Notes

How do I flash the CMOS?—The process of flashing a computer's CMOS is dangerous for the computer. If the CMOS is flashed with the incorrect BIOS update or is interrupted during the flash, the data on the EEPROM chip could be lost or corrupted and render the system BIOS useless. For this reason there is no lab exercise that allows you to flash a workstation's BIOS.

A+ CERTIFICATION OBJECTIVES

Table 2-1   Core A+ Objectives

Objectives	Chapters	Page Numbers
1.1 Identify basic terms, concepts, and functions of system modules, including how each module should work during normal operation.	1, 2, 11, 15	
G. Boot process	2	74
H. BIOS	1	21, 25
I. CMOS	1	8
1.8 Identify concepts and procedures relating to BIOS.	2, 3	
A. Methods for upgrading	2, 3	89, 138-140
B. When to upgrade	3	135-136,138-140
4.4 Identify the purpose of CMOS (Complementary Metal-Oxide Semiconductor), what it contains and how to change its basic parameters.	3, 9, Appendix B	
A. Example Basic CMOS Settings:	3	159-160
1. **Printer parallel port**	9	469-471
a. Uni., bi-directional,	9	469-471
b. disable/enable,	9	469-471
c. ECP, EPP	9	469-471
2. **COM/serial port**	3	159, 160
a. memory address,	9	462, 463
b. interrupt request,	9	462, 463
c. disable	9	462, 463
3. **Floppy drive**	3	159, 160
a. enable/disable drive or boot,	3	159, 160
b. speed,	3	159, 160
c. density	3	159, 160
4. **Hard drive size and drive type**	3, Appendix B	159, 160, B-1, B-2
5. **Memory parity,**	3	159, 160
a. non-parity	3	159, 160
6. Boot sequence	3	159, 160
7. Date/Time	3	159, 160

Review Questions

Circle True or False.

1. A System Configuration Worksheet is used to record your operating system's configuration.
True / False

2. The system time and date are always configured through the CMOS SETUP program.
True / False

3. Always record your CMOS settings before making changes.   True / False

2

4. Describe some of the dangers of flashing a CMOS.

_____

_____

_____

_____

_____

5. You are employed at the Yesterday Company as a desktop PC support technician. Karl, a coworker, has added a hard drive to a computer. Karl verified that the hard drive is properly connected and powered, but the computer still won't recognize the drive. What recommendations can you give Karl?

_____

_____

_____

_____

_____

6. You just finished installing 32MB of RAM into Umair's computer for him. You now want to verify that Umair's computer recognizes all 32MB of RAM. Describe below how you can verify the memory configuration on Umair's computer.

_____

_____

_____

_____

_____

Lab 2.2 IRQ and DMA Management

Objective

The objective of this lab is to provide you with the necessary experience of viewing currently installed device drivers, modifying their IRQ, DMA, and I/O address settings, and developing a general understanding of resource allocations. After completing this lab exercise, you will be able to:

- List examples of standard IRQ and DMA usage.

- Explain how to determine which IRQ and DMA channels and addresses are being utilized.

- Explain how to modify IRQ and DMA address settings to resolve resource conflicts.

- Identify installed device drivers in the Windows 9x environment.

Materials Required

One Windows 9x lab workstation for every four students. The lab workstations should meet the following requirements:

- 486 or better

- At least 16MB of RAM

- 540MB or larger hard drive

Lab Setup & Safety Tips

- Each lab workstation should have Windows 9x installed and functioning properly.

Activity

Recording your lab workstation's IRQ settings

1. Start your lab workstation, and allow it to boot into Windows 9x.

2. Click the **Start** button.

3. Point to **Settings**.

4. Click **Control Panel**.

5. Double-click the **System** icon.

6. Click the **Device Manager** tab.

7. Click the **Properties** button.

8. Record the device name for each of the following IRQs:

IRQ 00 _____

IRQ 01 _____

IRQ 02 _____

IRQ 03 _____

IRQ 04 _____

IRQ 05 _____

IRQ 06 _____

IRQ 07 _____

IRQ 08 _____

2

IRQ 09 _____

IRQ 10 _____

IRQ 11 _____

IRQ 12 _____

IRQ 13 _____

IRQ 14 _____

IRQ 15 _____

Recording your lab workstation's DMA settings

1. Start your lab workstation, and allow it to boot into Windows 9x.

2. Click the **Start** button.

3. Point to **Settings**.

4. Click **Control Panel**.

5. Double-click on the **System** icon.

6. Click the **Device Manager** tab.

7. Click the **Properties** button.

8. Click the **Direct Memory Access (DMA)** option button.

9. Record the device name for each of the following DMA channels:

DMA 01 _____

DMA 02 _____

DMA 03 _____

DMA 04 _____

Lab Notes

Device Manager—Device Manager is a Windows 9x program that you can use to view all of the currently installed device drivers and their resource configuration.

What is an IRQ?—An IRQ is a number that is assigned to a device and is used to signal the CPU for servicing.

What is a DMA?—A DMA controller chip is a chip that resides on the system-board and provides channels that a device may use to bypass the CPU and send data directly to memory.

CERTIFICATION OBJECTIVES

Table 2-2 Core A+ Objectives

Objectives	Chapters	Page Numbers
1.3 Identify available IRQs, DMAs, and I/O addresses and procedures for configuring them for device installation.	2, 5, 7, 9	
A. Standard IRQ settings	2, 9	83, 90, 463

Table 2-3 DOS/Windows A+ Objectives

Objectives	Chapters	Page Numbers
1.2 Identify ways to navigate the operating system and how to get to needed technical information.	1, 12	
A. Procedures (e.g., menu or icon - driven) for navigating through DOS to perform such things as locating, accessing, and retrieving information.	1	44
B. Procedures for navigating through the Windows 3.x/Windows 95 operating system, accessing, and retrieving information.	1, 12	49, 50, 600, 601

Review Questions

Circle True or False.

1. The Device Manager utility can be used to view all of the DMA channels and the devices currently configured to use them.   True / False

2. Device Manager is located on the Control Panel and accessed through the Add New Hardware icon.   True / False

3. IRQ stand for internal response question.   True / False

4. DMA stands for direct memory access.   True / False

5. You are employed as a hardware technician at Crunchy Com Corporation. One of your coworkers, Todd, just finished installing a modem into a customer's computer. Unfortunately, the modem doesn't seem to be functioning properly. Todd believes there is a resource conflict between the modem and another device. Todd asks you for help because he is new to the Windows 9x environment. Write the steps you would take to help Todd discover the resource conflict.

_____

_____

_____

_____

_____

6. Consult your list of IRQs. Which device is IRQ 15 normally reserved for?

_____

_____

_____

_____

_____

LAB 2.3 I/O MANAGEMENT

Objective

The objective of this lab is to provide you with experience managing I/O addresses, and resolving conflicts between I/O addresses. After completing this lab exercise, you will be able to:

- Explain the importance of unique I/O addresses.
- Determine which I/O addresses are being utilized.
- Identify and resolve an I/O address conflict.
- Install a network interface card.

Materials Required

One Windows 9x lab workstation for every four students. The lab workstations should meet the following requirements:

- 486 or better
- At least 16MB of RAM
- 540MB or larger hard drive

One network interface card that will be used to create a conflict with an assigned I/O address

One ESD mat for each lab workstation

Grounding straps for each student

The necessary tools for removing the system unit's case and adding a network interface card

One network interface card for each lab workstation (*Note:* This card should not be installed at the beginning of the lab exercise.)

Documentation for the network interface card, including jumper settings

Lab Setup & Safety Tips

- Each lab workstation should have Windows 9x installed and functioning properly.
- Each group of students should have one network interface card in an ESD safe bag and documentation that describes the proper jumper settings for the card.
- Always verify that the power cord is removed from the PC before touching any component inside the computer's case.

ACTIVITY

Creating the I/O address conflict

Your instructor will tell you at which I/O address you will be creating a conflict.

1. Start your lab workstation, and allow it to boot into Windows 9x.
2. Click the **Start** button.
3. Point to **Settings**.
4. Click **Control Panel**.
5. Double-click the **System** icon.
6. Click the **Device Manager** tab.
7. Click the **Properties** button.

8. Click the **I/O (Input/Output)** option button.

9. Observe the current device configurations of the predetermined I/O address.

10. Click the **Cancel** button.

11. Close Device Manager and shut down Windows.

12. Verify that you are properly grounded.

13. Unplug the power cord from the system unit.

14. Remove the top of the case.

15. Locate the available slot where you plan to install the network interface card.

16. Using the provided documentation, verify that the network interface card is configured to use the predetermined I/O address and an available IRQ.

17. Gently install the network interface card into the slot. *Warning*: Don't bend the card from side to side; move the card only back and forth from end to end.

18. Screw the mounting screw into place.

19. Replace the top of the case.

20. Plug in the system unit.

21. Power on the lab workstation, and allow it to boot into Windows 9x.

22. If the workstation fails to boot properly, power cycle the PC, and, when prompted, choose **Safe Mode**.

Observing the I/O conflict

1. Start your lab workstation, and allow it to boot into Windows 9x.

2. Click the **Start** button.

3. Point to **Settings**.

4. Click **Control Panel**.

5. Double-click the **System** icon.

6. Click the **Device Manager** tab.

7. Double-click the icon of the installed network card.

8. Click the **Resources** tab.

9. Observe the conflicting device list.

10. Click the **Cancel** button.

11. Close Device Manager and shut down Windows.

Resolving the I/O conflict

Your instructor will provide you with an available I/O address.

1. Unplug the power cord from the system unit.

2. Remove the top of the case.

3. Locate the network interface card.

4. Using the provided documentation, configure the network interface card to use the I/O address specified by your instructor.

5. Replace the top of the case.

6. Plug in the system unit.

7. Power on the lab workstation, and allow it to boot into Windows 9x.

8. If the workstation fails to boot properly, power cycle the PC, and, when prompted, choose **Safe Mode**.

>
> ### Lab Notes
> **What is power cycle?**—The term power cycle refers to turning off and on the power to your PC.
>
> **What is an I/O address?**—An I/O address is an address stored in RAM assigned to the operations of a particular device.

A+ CERTIFICATION OBJECTIVES

Table 2-4   Core A+ Objectives

Objectives	Chapters	Page Numbers
1.3 Identify available IRQs, DMAs, and I/O addresses and procedures for configuring them for device installation.	2, 5, 7, 9	
A. Standard IRQ settings	2, 9	83, 90, 463
2.2 Identify basic troubleshooting procedures and good practices for eliciting problem symptoms from customers.	8, Appendix A	
A. Troubleshooting/isolation/problem determination procedures.	8	416-420
B. Determine whether hardware or software problem.	8	416-420
E. Symptoms/Error Codes	8, Appendix A	416-420, A1, A2
F. Situation when the problem occurred	8	416-421

Review Questions

Circle True or False.

1. Only two devices at a time can use an I/O address.   True / False

2. I/O stands for input/output.   True / False

3. An I/O address is a physical location on the hard drive where the CPU will store data. True / False

4. Almost all hardware devices need at least six I/O addresses to function properly.   True / False

5. Describe the steps you would take to determine which hardware device or devices are conflicting with a particular component.

   _____

   _____

   _____

   _____

   _____

6. You have recently installed a new network interface card. You believe that its I/O address is conflicting with your sound card. Describe two ways you could quickly resolve this conflict without removing either component.

   _____

   _____

   _____

   _____

   _____

LAB 2.4 THE BOOT PROCESS

Objective

The objective of this lab exercise is to familiarize you with the boot process of a PC and to provide hands-on troubleshooting experience. After completing this lab exercise, you will be able to:

- Describe, in order, the PC boot process.
- Describe the effect that various defective components have on the boot process.
- Troubleshoot the PC boot process.

Materials Required

One Windows 9x lab workstation for every four students. The lab workstations should meet the following requirements:

- 486 or better
- At least 16MB of RAM
- 540MB or larger hard drive

One ESD mat for each lab workstation

Grounding straps for each student

Necessary tools for removing the system unit's case

Lab Setup & Safety Tips

- Each lab workstation should have Window 9x installed and functioning properly.

ACTIVITY

Observing the boot process

1. Turn on your PC.
2. Note the various startup screens.
3. Shut down your PC.
4. Verify that you are properly grounded.
5. Unplug the power cord from the system unit.
6. Remove the case.
7. Remove all of the SIMMS from your PC.
8. Restart your PC.
9. Record the effect of removing the SIMMS:

   _____

10. Shut down your PC.
11. Reinstall the SIMMs that you removed in Step 7.
12. Restart your PC.
13. Note the effect of replacing the SIMMS.
14. Shut down your PC.
15. Reverse the hard drive cable at the systemboard.

2

16. Restart your PC.

17. Record the effect of reversing the hard drive cabling:

    _____

18. Shut down your PC.

19. Correctly install the hard drive cable at the systemboard.

20. Remove the hard drive cable from the hard drive.

21. Restart your PC.

22. Record the effect of the uninstalled hard drive cable:

    _____

23. Shut down your PC.

24. Reinstall the hard drive cable at the hard drive.

25. Restart your PC.

26. Note the effect of the installed hard drive cable.

27. Shut down your PC.

28. Remove the floppy drive cable from the systemboard.

29. Restart your PC.

30. Record the effect of the uninstalled floppy drive cable:

    _____

31. Shut down your PC.

32. Reinstall the floppy drive cable.

33. Restart your PC.

34. Note the effect of the installed floppy drive cable.

35. Shut down your PC.

36. Remove the keyboard from the PC.

37. Restart your PC.

38. Record the effect of the uninstalled keyboard:

    _____

39. Shut down your PC.

40. Reinstall the keyboard.

41. Restart your PC.

42. Note the effect of the installed keyboard.

 Lab Notes

What is POST?—POST stands for power-on self-test. POST is a self-diagnostic program used to perform a simple test of the CPU, RAM, and various I/O devices. The POST is performed when the computer is first powered on.

A+   ## CERTIFICATION OBJECTIVES

Table 2-5   Core A+ Objectives

Objectives	Chapters	Page Numbers
1.1 Identify basic terms, concepts, and functions of system modules, including how each module should work during normal operation.	1, 2, 11, 15	
A. System board	1	9
D. Memory	1	21
G. Boot process	2	74
1.2 Identify basic procedures for adding and removing field replaceable modules.	1, 3, 4, 11, 17	
E. Memory	1, 4, 14	11, 228-229, 764, 766
2.1 Identify common symptoms and problems associated with each module and how to troubleshoot and isolate the problems	2, 3, 5, 7, 8, 10, 11, 15 Appendices A and E	
A. Processor/Memory symptoms	3, 8, Appendix E	122, 130, 131, 425
B. Mouse	9, Appendix E	489-491, E11
C. Floppy drive failures	5, Appendix E	262-267, E9
D. Hard Drives	7, Appendix E	362-364, 381-384, E1
4.4 Identify the purpose of CMOS (Complementary Metal-Oxide Semiconductor), what it contains and how to change its basic parameters.	3, 9, Appendix B	
4. **Hard drive size and drive type**	3, Appendix B	159, 160, B1, B2
5. **Memory parity,**	3	159, 160
a. non-parity	3	159, 160
6. **Boot sequence**	3	159, 160

Review Questions

Circle **True** or **False**.

1. A PC can function properly without any memory installed.   **True / False**

2. Hard drive data cables are reversible.   **True / False**

3. Floppy drive data cables are not reversible.   **True / False**

4. If a PC is started without a keyboard attached, you will receive an error message during the POST.   **True / False**

5. The absence of what single component from the previous activity will halt all system activities?

   _____

   _____

   _____

   _____

6. You just finished moving a PC from one building to another. You have not changed any of the PC's hardware configurations, but now when you start the system it gives you a keyboard/mouse error. If the keyboard and mouse are plugged in, what could be the problem?

   _____

   _____

   _____

   _____

3

THE SYSTEMBOARD

LABS INCLUDED IN THIS CHAPTER

♦ **LAB 3.1** **COMPONENT IDENTIFICATION**

♦ **LAB 3.2** **CPU IDENTIFICATION AND INSTALLATION**

♦ **LAB 3.3** **BUS IDENTIFICATION AND PCI EXPANSION CARD INSTALLATION**

LAB 3.1 COMPONENT IDENTIFICATION

Objective

The objective of this lab exercise is to provide you with the ability to identify various components of the systemboard from several different generations of personal computers. After completing this lab exercise, you will be able to:

- Identify the major components of systemboards from different generations.

Materials Required

One Windows 9x lab workstation for every four students. The lab workstations should meet the following requirements:

- 486 or better

- At least 16MB of RAM

- 540MB or larger hard drive

Systemboard documentation for each of the lab workstations. You should be able to identify the location and purpose of each jumper block on the systemboard.

Each group of students will require a packet of labels.

Any available systemboards from each of the following generations:

- PC
- PC-AT
- 286
- 386
- 486
- Pentium
- Pentium Pro
- Pentium II

Lab Setup & Safety Tips

To create the instructor's display, arrange the available systemboards with the following components labeled:

- ISA expansion bus
- PCI expansion bus
- VLB expansion bus
- Bus control chip set
- System BIOS
- Keyboard BIOS
- Battery
- DRAM
- SIMMS
- DIMMS

- Keyboard connector
- Mouse connector
- Cache memory
- Integrated IDE controller
- Integrated floppy drive controller
- Integrated I/O connectors
- Power supply
- RAM slots
- CPU socket

ACTIVITY

Viewing the instructor's display

1. Record at least one hardware difference between each of the systemboard generations.

PC _____

_____

_____

PC–AT _____

_____

_____

_____

286 _____

_____

_____

386 _____

_____

_____

486 _____

_____

_____

Pentium I _____

_____

_____

Pentium Pro _____

_____

_____

Pentium II _____

_____

_____

Labeling the lab workstation

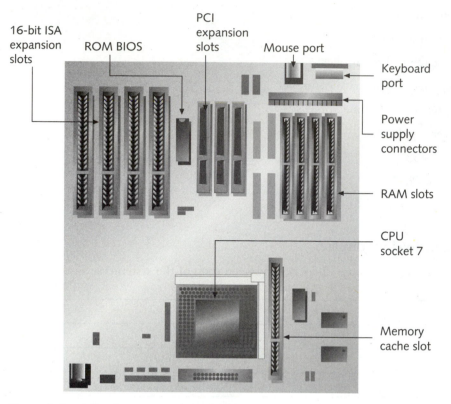

Figure 3-1   A Pentium systemboard with no components added

Labeling your workstation components

1. Label each component of your lab workstation as shown above.

Labeling the jumper blocks

1. Refer to the provided documentation and label each of your lab workstation's jumper blocks.

Table 3-1   Major manufacturers of systemboards

Manufacturer	Product	Web Address
Acer America Corp.	Pentium boards	www.acer.com
American Megatrends	486, Pentium boards	www.megatrends.com
ASUS	486, Pentium boards	www.asus.com
First International Computer, Inc.	486, Pentium boards	www.fica.com
Giga-Byte Technology, Co.	Pentium boards	www.giga-byte.com
Intel Corporation	Pentium boards	www.intel.com
Micronics Computers	Pentium boards	www.micronics.com
Ocean Office Automation, Ltd.	486, Pentium boards	www.ocean-usa.com
Supermicro Computers, Inc.	Pentium boards	www.supermicro.com
Tyan Computer	Pentium boards	www.tyan.com

Table 3-2   The Intel chip set family

Common Name	Model Number	Comments
Triton I	430FX	The oldest chip set, no longer produced
Triton II	430HX	High performance, supports dual CPUs
Triton III	430VX 430MX 430TX	Value chip set, supports SDRAM Used for notebooks (M=mobile) Supports SDRAM, ultra DMA; replaces the VX and MX
Natoma	440FX	Supports Pentium Pro and Pentium II
Orion	450GX, KX	Supports Pentium Pro

A^+ ## CERTIFICATION OBJECTIVES

Table 3-3   Core A+ Objectives

Objectives	Chapters	Page Numbers
1.1 Identify basic terms, concepts, and functions of system modules, including how each module should work during normal operation.	1, 2, 11, 15	
A. System board	1	9
B. Power supply	1, 11	19, 575, 576
C. Processor /CPU	1	4, 10
D. Memory	1	21
H. BIOS	1	21, 25
I. CMOS	1	8
1.2 Identify basic procedures for adding and removing field replaceable modules.	1, 3, 4, 11, 14	
A. System board	1	14
B. Storage device	1, 14	11, 774-779
C. Power supply	1, 11, 14	19, 575, 576, 766-771
D. Processor /CPU	3, 14	115, 760, 763
E. Memory	1, 4, 14	11, 228-229, 764, 766
F. Input devices	1, 14	5, 14, 780-782
4.3 Identify the most popular type of motherboards, their components, and their architecture (for example, bus structures and power supplies).	2, 3, 4, 9, 17	
A. **Types of motherboards:**		
1. AT (Full and Baby)	3	114
2. ATX	3	114
B. **Components:**		
1. Communication ports	9	462, 463
2. SIMM AND DIMM	3	142
3. Processor sockets	3	130-132
4. External cache memory (Level 2)	3, 4	124, 181

Table 3-3 Core A+ Objectives (continued)

Objectives		Chapters	Page Numbers
C.	**Bus Architecture**	3	121
1.	ISA	2, 3	81, 144, 148, 150, 151
2.	EISA	3	145, 148
3.	PCI	3	145, 146, 149, 151
4.	USB (Universal Serial Bus)	3	145, 146, 148, 149
5.	VESA local bus (VL-Bus)	3	145-146, 151
6.	PC Card (PCMCIA)	17	969
D.	**Basic compatibility guidelines**	17	969

Review Questions

Circle True or False.

1. The mouse and keyboard ports are always located directly next to the CPU socket.
   True / False

2. Systemboards require two power connectors from the power supply.   True / False

3. Different systemboards can use different types of memory.   True / False

4. ISA slots are shorter in length than PCI slots.   True / False

5. Most CPUs are bolted to the systemboard to prevent them from slipping off and causing the entire PC to crash.   True / False

6. What does the acronym USB stand for?

   _____

7. You are employed at Cold Sweet Ice Company as a helpdesk technician. Jamie, one of your favorite customers, wants to install more memory into her PC but doesn't know how to attach it to the systemboard. Describe below the steps Jamie needs to follow to locate the memory slots.

   _____
   _____
   _____
   _____
   _____

LAB 3.2 CPU IDENTIFICATION AND INSTALLATION

Objective

The objective of this lab exercise is to enable you to identify the various central processing units (CPUs), or microprocessors, and their corresponding mounting technologies from different generations of personal computers. After completing this lab exercise, you will be able to:

- Identify the various generations of CPUs, or microprocessors, used in PCs.
- Identify the various generations of CPU mounting technology used in PCs.
- Install and remove a 486 CPU.

Materials Required

One Windows 9x lab workstation for every four students. The lab workstations should meet the following requirements:

- 486 or better
- At least 16MB of RAM
- 540MB or larger hard drive

One grounding strap for each student

One chip pulling tool for each lab workstation

One grounding mat for each lab workstation

Any available CPUs from each of the following families:

- 8088
- 80286
- 80386
- 80486
- Pentium
- Pentium Pro
- Pentium II
- Pentium III

Lab Setup & Safety Tips

- Each lab workstation should have Windows 9x installed and functioning properly.
- Arrange the CPUs and the matching mounting technology, labeling each so that other students can inspect them.
- Always unplug the power cord before touching any component within the case.

ACTIVITY

Viewing the instructor's display

1. Inspect each of the available CPUs, and note their characteristics.
2. Also note the mounting technology associated with the respective CPUs, and the mounting technology characteristics.

Removing your workstation's CPU

1. Power off your lab workstation.

2. Unplug the system unit's power cord.

3. Verify that you are properly grounded.

4. Remove the case from your lab workstation.

5. Locate the CPU.

6. If the computer has a heat sink, release the heat sink from the top of the CPU (if the heat sink doesn't come off with ease, leave it on top of the CPU).

7. Release the ZIF lever.

8. Note how the CPU is currently installed. This will be important when you try to reinstall the CPU. Specifically note the orientation of the writing on the CPU.

9. Use the chip pulling tool to remove your CPU. *Warning*: When removing your CPU, pull evenly straight up on the CPU; do not bend it from side to side.

10. Stand clear of the case and plug in the power cord.

11. Power on the PC and observe the results of a PC without a CPU.

Reinstalling your workstation's CPU

1. Power off the workstation.

2. Remember which direction the CPU should be facing and gently slide it back into the correct position.

3. Don't force the CPU. If it is not moving into place with ease, check for bent pins on the bottom of the CPU.

4. Lock the CPU into position using the ZIF lever.

5. If necessary, replace the heat sink on top of the CPU.

6. Test the installation before replacing the case.

7. Stand clear of the case and plug in the power cord.

8. Power on the PC and verify that the system boots properly.

9. Power off the PC and unplug the power cord.

10. Replace the case.

11. Plug in the system unit.

12. Power on the system unit.

13. Power off the PC.

3

Lab Notes

How do I control the CPU settings?—Most CPU's are configured using jumper blocks or DIP switches located directly on the systemboard.

Do I always need a heat sink?—Any CPU, starting with a 486 and moving up, requires a heat sink to maintain proper CPU temperature.

What is the correct voltage for my CPU?—CPU voltage varies depending on the brand name and generation of the CPU. Consult the documentation for your CPU

Table 3-4   The Intel Pentium family of chips

Processor	Current Clock Speeds	MMX	Primary Cache
Classic Pentium	100, 120, 133, 150, 166, 200	No	16K
Pentium MMX	150, 166, 200	Yes	32K
Pentium Pro	166, 180, 200	No	16K
Pentium II	166, 180, 200, 266, 300	Yes	32K
Deschutes	Expecting 300, 333, 400	Yes	Unknown

 CERTIFICATION OBJECTIVES

Table 3-5   Core A+ Objectives

Objectives	Chapters	Page Numbers
1.1 Identify basic terms, concepts, and functions of system modules, including how each module should work during normal operation.	1, 2, 11, 15	
A. System board	1	9
C. Processor/CPU	1	4, 10
1.2 Identify basic procedures for adding and removing field replaceable modules.	1, 3, 4, 11, 14	
A. System board	1	14
D. Processor/CPU	3, 14	115, 760, 763
1.8 Identify concepts and procedures relating to BIOS.	2, 3	
A. Methods for upgrading	2, 3	89, 138-140
B. When to upgrade	3	135-136, 138-140
4.1 Distinguish between the popular CPU chips in terms of their basic characteristics.	3	
A. Popular CPU chips Characteristics:	3	120, 121, 123, 125-128
1. Physical size	3	130-132
2. Voltage	3	122
3. Speeds	3	123-129, 134, 135
4. On board cache	3	120
5. Sockets	3	128, 130-132
6. Number of pins	3	131

Review Questions

Circle True or False.

1. All CPUs are the same size.   True / False

2. CPU voltage varies depending on the generation and brand name.   True / False

3. Chip pullers are used to remove the heat sink from the top of the CPU.   True / False

4. ZIF sockets are used to connect the memory to the systemboard.   True / False

5. Which is faster: the 8088 processor or the 486 processor?

   _____

   _____

6. You are currently employed as a PC support technician at the Heavenly Palace Factory. Your supervisor wants to upgrade his 486 computer to a Pentium 166. He has asked you to tell him the parts that he will need to purchase for this upgrade. List below the minimum parts your supervisor needs to complete this upgrade.

   _____

   _____

   _____

   _____

   _____

7. You are at your local computer store and are considering upgrading your home PC to a Pentium Pro. Will you be able to use the CPU cooling fan from your 486 at home if you purchase the Pentium Pro chip?

   _____

   _____

   _____

   _____

   _____

LAB 3.3 BUS IDENTIFICATION AND PCI EXPANSION CARD INSTALLATION

Objective

The objective of this lab exercise is to provide a hands-on opportunity to view and identify the different types of PC expansion buses. After completing this lab exercise, you will be able to:

- Identify the various expansion buses used in PCs.
- Describe the various components of the respective expansion buses.
- Install a PCI expansion card.

Materials Required

One Windows 9x lab workstation for every four students. The lab workstations should meet the following requirements:

- 486 or better
- At least 16MB of RAM
- 540MB or larger hard drive

One PCI expansion card of any kind

One ESD mat for every lab workstation

One grounding strap for each student

Any available systemboards from each of the following generations:

- PC
- PC-AT
- IBM PC
- 286
- 386
- 486
- Pentium
- Pentium II

Lab Setup & Safety Tips

- Each lab workstation should have Windows 9x installed and functioning properly.
- Arrange the systemboards with their respective expansion buses and corresponding control chip sets so that students can inspect them.
- Students must comply with standard ESD procedures.
- Always unplug the power cord before touching any component within the case.

ACTIVITY

Getting to know expansion buses

1. Inspect and note the characteristics of the following architectures:

   - ISA 8-bit expansion bus
   - ISA 16-bit expansion bus
   - VLB expansion bus and its control chip set
   - PCI expansion bus and its control chip set
   - MCA expansion bus and its control chip set

2. After the labels on the display are removed and then rearranged, match the labels to their corresponding expansion buses.

Installing a PCI expansion card

1. Power off your PC.

2. Verify that you are properly grounded.

3. Unplug the system unit's power cord.

4. Remove the top of the case.

5. Locate the available PCI slot where you plan to install the PCI expansion card.

6. Gently install the PCI expansion card into the slot. *Warning*: Don't bend the card from side to side; move the card only back and forth or from end to end.

7. Screw the mounting screw into place.

8. Replace the top of the case.

9. Plug in the system unit.

10. Power on the lab workstation and allow it to boot into Windows 9x.

Removing the PCI expansion card

1. Power off your PC.

2. Verify that you are properly grounded.

3. Unplug the system unit's power cord.

4. Remove the top of the case.

5. Unscrew the mounting screw from the frame.

6. Gently remove the PCI expansion card from the PCI slot. *Warning*: Don't bend the card from side to side; move the card only back and forth or from end to end.

7. Replace the top of the case.

8. Plug in the system unit.

9. Power on the lab workstation, and allow it to boot into Windows 9x.

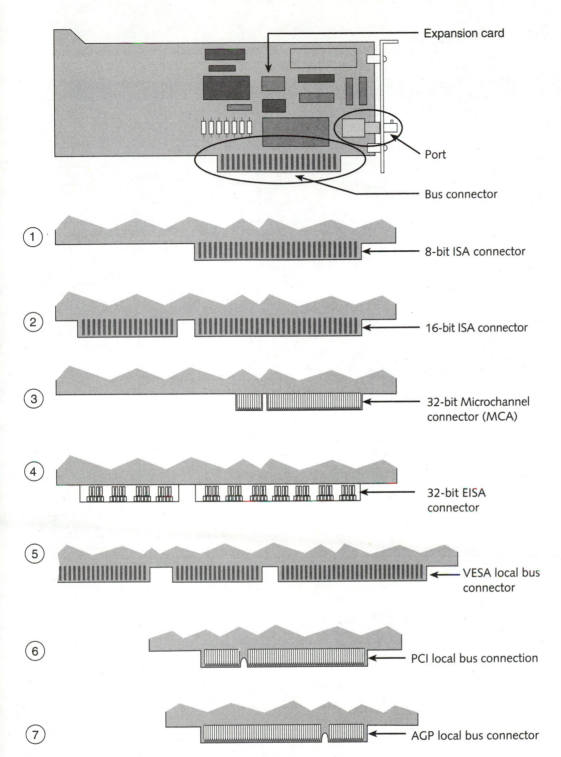

Figure 3-2   Seven bus connections on expansion cards

A+ CERTIFICATION OBJECTIVES

Table 3-6   Core A+ Objectives

Objectives	Chapters	Page Numbers
4.3 Identify the most popular type of motherboards, their components, and their architecture (for example, bus structures and power supplies).	2, 3, 4, 9 17	
C. Bus Architecture	3	121
1. ISA	2, 3	81, 144, 148, 150, 151
2. EISA	3	145, 148
3. PCI	3	145, 146, 149, 151
4. USB (Universal Serial Bus)	3	145, 146, 148, 149
5. VESA local bus (VL-Bus)	3	145, 146, 151
6. PC Card (PCMCIA)	17	969

Review Questions

Circle True or False.

1. ISA is always faster than PCI.   True / False

2. Microchannel is a 64-bit bus.   True / False

3. Microchannel and EISA can use the same expansion slot.   True / False

4. An ISA expansion card can be either 8-bit or 16-bit.   True / False

5. John wants to add a sound card to his 386. Before purchasing the sound card, he is going to look at his systemboard to find out what type he should purchase. Describe to John how to tell if he has an 8-bit or a 16-bit ISA expansion slot on his systemboard.

   _____

   _____

   _____

   _____

   _____

6. What is one advantage of using PCI over ISA?

   _____

   _____

   _____

   _____

   _____

UNDERSTANDING AND MANAGING MEMORY

LABS INCLUDED IN THIS CHAPTER

Lab 4.1 Installing RAM and Understanding the CONFIG.SYS

Objective

The objective of this lab exercise is to teach you how to properly install RAM and to understand the differences between the kinds of RAM currently sold on the market. After completing this lab exercise you will be able to:

- Install RAM.
- Write and modify a CONFIG.SYS file.
- Describe features of different types of RAM.

Materials Required

This lab exercise requires one complete lab workstation for every four students. The lab workstation should meet the following requirements:

- 486 or better
- 16MB of RAM
- Windows 9x
- One 4MB or larger RAM chip

One ESD mat for each lab workstation

Grounding straps for each student

Lab Setup & Safety Tips

- Each lab workstation should have both Windows 9x and DOS 5.0 or greater installed and functioning properly.
- Students must comply with standard ESD procedures.
- Always unplug the power cord before touching any component within the case.

Activity

Installing RAM

1. Power off the lab workstation.
2. Unplug the power cord.
3. Remove the case from the lab workstation.
4. Locate the SIMM banks on your systemboard.
5. Place the SIMM at a 45-degree angle and then gently snap it into place.
6. After the SIMM has been installed, replace the case.
7. Plug in the power cord.
8. Power on your lab workstation.
9. Enter the CMOS Setup program.
10. Verify that the Setup program recognizes the correct amount of memory.
11. Save the changes and reboot the workstation.
12. Allow your lab workstation to boot into Windows 9x.

13. Right-click the **My Computer** icon.

14. Select **Properties** from the shortcut menu.

15. On the General tab, locate the Computer heading.

16. Verify that Windows 9x is using all of the installed memory.

Recording the characteristics of RAM

In the following section, write the definition for each type of RAM; be sure to include how each type is used and any of its advantages or disadvantages. You will find the definitions in the text-book on pages 178 through 186.

SRAM

_____

_____

_____

_____

_____

DRAM

_____

_____

_____

_____

DIMMS

_____

_____

_____

_____

Parity RAM

_____

_____

_____

_____

Nonparity RAM

_____

_____

_____

_____

EDO RAM

_____

_____

_____

_____

_____

FPM RAM

_____

_____

_____

_____

Flash Memory

_____

_____

_____

_____

_____

SDRAM

_____

_____

_____

_____

_____

COAST

_____

_____

_____

_____

_____

Examining the CONFIG.SYS

1. Allow your lab workstation to boot to DOS.

2. At the command prompt in the root directory, type **EDIT CONFIG.SYS** and press **Enter**. Your lab workstation should respond by launching the EDIT program and opening the CONFIG.SYS file.

On the following lines copy the contents of your CONFIG.SYS; then next to each command, write how your lab workstation should respond. You will find the command definitions in the textbook on pages 198 through 208.

Example:

BUFFERS=40 – This command tells DOS how many buffers to maintain when transferring data to and from secondary storage.

_____

_____

_____

_____

_____

_____

_____

_____

_____

_____

_____

_____

_____

_____

_____

_____

_____

_____

_____

_____

> ### Lab Notes
>
> **What is conventional memory?**—Conventional memory, or base memory, is the first 640K of RAM.
>
> **What is upper memory?**—Upper memory includes memory addresses starting at 641K and going up to 1024K.
>
> **What is extended memory?**—Memory addresses above 1024K are referred to as residing in extended memory.
>
> **What is expanded memory?**—Expanded memory is memory that falls outside the linear memory addressing scheme. Note that expanded memory normally is accessed via upper memory. Refer to textbook page 195 for more information about expanded memory.
>
> **What is virtual memory?**—Virtual memory is an area of secondary storage that is set aside to be used as an area of RAM. Note that because it is secondary storage the access time is considerably slower than that of RAM.

CERTIFICATION OBJECTIVES

Table 4-1   Core A+ Objectives

Objectives	Chapters	Page Numbers
4.2 Identify the categories of RAM (Random Access Memory) terminology, their locations, and physical characteristics.	3, 4, 9	
A. Terminology:		
1. EDO RAM (Extended Data Output RAM)	3, 4	142, 181, 185
2. DRAM (Dynamic Random Access Memory)	3, 4	124, 141-143, 178, 181
3. SRAM (Static RAM)	3, 4	124, 141, 181
4. VRAM (Video RAM)	9	500
5. WRAM (Windows Accelerator Card RAM)	9	500, 501
B. Locations and physical characteristics:		
1. Memory bank	4	178
2. Memory chips (8-bit, 16-bit, and 32-bit)	4	186
3. SIMMS (Single In-line Memory Module)	3, 4	142, 184
4. DIMMS (Dual In-line Memory Module)	3, 4	142, 185
5. Parity chips versus non-parity chips	3, 4	141, 186-187

Table 4-2   DOS/Windows A+ Objectives

Objectives	Chapters	Page Numbers
2.1 Differentiate between types of memory.	1, 4	
A. Conventional	4	192, 193
B. Extended/upper memory	4	192-194
C. High memory	4	192, 193
D. Expanded memory	4	192, 193, 195, 196
E. Virtual memory	1, 4	42, 196

Review Questions

Circle True or False.

1. When you install memory into a PC, the memory must always be installed in pairs.
   True / False

2. Conventional memory includes the first 128K of RAM.   True / False

3. EDO stands for "extended data output."   True / False

4. EDO RAM is faster than FPM RAM.   True / False

5. Flash memory is commonly used as a cache for desktop PCs.   True / False

6. If the following line were added to your CONFIG.SYS file, what would it tell your computer to do?

   DEVICE=C:\DOS\HIMEM.SYS

   _____

   _____

   _____

   _____

7. What would the following command tell your PC to do?
   EDIT AUTOEXEC.BAT

   _____

   _____

   _____

   _____

   _____

4

LAB 4.2 MEMORY MANAGEMENT IN DOS AND WINDOWS 3.X

Objective

The objective of this lab exercise is to make you familiar with some common methods of memory management available in the DOS and Windows 3.x environments. After completing this lab exercise, you will be able to:

- Load TSRs from either CONFIG.SYS or AUTOEXEC.BAT.
- Use the MEM command to view your workstation's current memory configuration.
- Create and modify a Windows 3.x swap file.

Materials Required

This lab exercise requires one complete lab workstation for every four students. The lab workstation should meet the following requirements:

- 486 or better
- 16MB of RAM
- Windows 3.x

One disk for each lab workstation containing a TSR

Lab Setup & Safety Tips

- Each lab workstation should have Windows 3.x installed and functioning properly.

ACTIVITY

Loading a TSR high

1. Allow your lab workstation to boot to DOS.
2. Insert the TSR disk provided by your instructor.
3. Use the COPY command to copy the TSR from the disk to the root directory of your lab workstation.
4. Make C:\ your current directory.
5. Type **EDIT AUTOEXEC.BAT** and press **Enter**.
6. Add the following to your AUTOEXEC.BAT file (note that the TSR.TSR should be replaced with the name of the TSR on the disk), **LH C:\TSR.TSR**.
7. Press the **Alt** key.
8. Use the down arrow [↓] to select **Save** from the File menu.
9. Press the **Alt** key.
10. Use the down arrow [↓] to select **Exit** from the File menu.
11. Reboot your lab workstation.
12. To verify that the TSR loaded, attempt to use its function.

Using the MEM command

Using the MEM command, complete the following table:

Memory Type	Total	Used	Free
Conventional memory			
Upper memory			
Reserved memory			
Extended memory			
Totals			
Total memory below 1 MB			

Configuring the swap file in the Windows 3.x environment

1. Allow your lab workstation to boot into Windows 3.1.

2. Double-click the **Main** group icon.

3. Double-click the **Control Panel** icon.

4. Double-click the **386 Enhanced** icon.

5. Click the **Virtual Memory** button.

6. Click the **Change** button.

7. Use the list arrow to change your swap file settings from Temporary to **Permanent**.

8. Click **OK**.

9. Click **Yes** when asked if you are sure you want to make changes to virtual memory settings.

10. Click the **Restart Windows** button.

Lab Notes

What is a TSR?—A TSR is any program or device driver that resides in memory even though it is not active. TSR stands for terminate and stay resident.

What is HIMEM.SYS?—HIMEM.SYS is a device driver used to manage expanded memory in the DOS and Windows 3.x environments. If HIMEM.SYS fails to load, reboot the PC and check your CONFIG.SYS to verify that the path is specified correctly.

How do I manage a corrupt swap file in Windows 3.x?—A corrupt swap file can be easily managed by booting into DOS, locating the swap file, and then deleting it. Restart the PC and allow it to boot into Windows 3.x. Use the 386 Enhanced icon in the Control Panel to create a new swap file.

A device referenced in the Win.ini could not be found—If you are receiving this error message, run the SYSEDIT utility and verify that all of your recently loaded drivers and files are using the correct path statements.

CERTIFICATION OBJECTIVES

Table 4-3   DOS/Windows A+ Objectives

Objectives	Chapters	Page Numbers
4.2 Identify the categories of RAM (Random Access Memory) terminology, their locations, and physical characteristics.		
2.2 Identify typical memory conflict problems and how to optimize memory use.	4, 12	
H. Himem.sys	4	204
4.1 Recognize and interpret the meaning of common error codes and startup messages from the boot sequence, and identify steps to correct the problems.	4, 5, 7, 8,12	
D. Error in CONFIG.SYS line XX	12	603
F. Himem.sys not loaded	4	198, 199
G. Missing or corrupt Himem.sys	4	198, 199
H. Swap file	4	217, 218
I. A device referenced in SYSTEM.INI could not be found	12	606, 607

Review Questions

Circle **True** or **False**.

1. TSR stands for terminate safety return. **True / False**

2. TSRs are programs that stay in memory even when they are not being used. **True / False**

3. TSRs can only be loaded into memory through the CONFIG.SYS. **True / False**

4. You can use the MEM command to view the amount of available hard drive space.
   True / False

5. The HIMEM.SYS file is used to test conventional memory. **True / False**

6. Which icon on the Control Panel do you double-click to modify the Window 3.x memory settings?

   _____

   _____

   _____

   _____

   _____

7. Describe how to manage a corrupt swap file in Windows 3.x.

   _____

   _____

   _____

   _____

   _____

Lab 4.3 Memory Management in Windows 9x

Objective

The objective of this lab exercise is to teach you how to manage and control memory allocation in the Windows 9x environment. After completing this lab exercise, you will be able to:

- Configure the Windows 9x swap file.
- Describe the advantages and disadvantages of using a swap file in Windows 9x.

Materials Required

This lab exercise requires one complete lab workstation for every four students. The lab workstation should meet the following requirements:

- 486 or better
- 16MB of RAM
- Windows 9x

Lab Setup & Safety Tips

- Each lab workstation should have Windows 9x installed and functioning properly.

Activity

Disabling the Windows 9x swap file

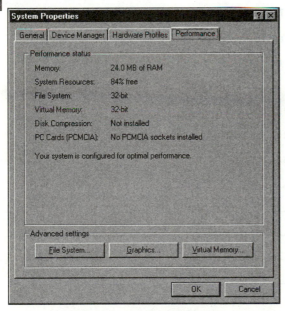

Figure 4-1 System Properties box in Windows 9x

1. Allow your lab workstation to boot into Windows 9x.

2. Right-click the **My Computer** icon.

3. Select **Properties** from the shortcut menu.

4. Click the **Performance** tab.

5. Click the **Virtual Memory** button.

6. Click the **Let me specify my own virtual memory settings** option button.

7. Place a check mark in the **Disable virtual memory** check box.

8. Click **OK**.

9. Click the **Yes** button on the confirmation message.

10. Click the **Close** button.

11. Click **Yes** when you are prompted to restart your computer.

12. Observe and describe the results.

_____

_____

_____

_____

_____

Specifying a permanent swap file

1. Allow your lab workstation to boot into Windows 9x.

2. Right-click the **My Computer** icon.

3. Select **Properties** from the shortcut menu.

4. Click the **Performance** tab.

5. Click the **Virtual Memory** button.

6. Click the **Let me specify my own virtual memory settings** option button.

7. Clear the check mark from the **Disable virtual memory** check box.

8. Set the minimum swap file size to **150MB**.

9. Set the maximum swap file size to **150MB**.

10. Click **OK**.

11. Click the **Yes** button on the confirmation message.

12. Click **Yes** when you are prompted to restart your computer.

13. Observe and describe the results.

_____

_____

_____

_____

_____

Allowing Windows to manage its virtual memory

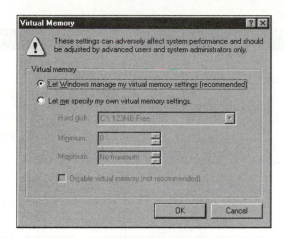

Figure 4-2   Options for managing virtual memory
in Windows 9x

1. Allow your lab workstation to boot into Windows 9x.

2. Right-click the **My Computer** icon.

3. Select **Properties** from the shortcut menu.

4. Click the **Performance** tab.

5. Click the **Virtual Memory** button.

6. Click the **Let Windows manage my virtual memory settings** option button.

7. Click the **OK** button on the Virtual Memory dialog box.

8. Click the **Yes** button if you receive a confirmation message.

9. Click the **Close** button.

10. Click **Yes** when you are prompted to restart your computer.

11. Observe and describe the results.

_____

_____

_____

_____

_____

Lab Notes

What is Windows doing when it manages my virtual memory?—By default, Windows 9x will manage your virtual memory. This means that it will size and resize your swap file as it sees fit. In most circumstances this is the recommended memory management method.

What is a memory conflict, and how does it occur?—A memory conflict occurs when two or more applications attempt to use the same memory address or address range.

What is an illegal operation?—These errors vary depending on the situation. You can find out exactly which applications were involved by clicking the Details button. Many times these errors are GPFs and should be handled accordingly.

CERTIFICATION OBJECTIVES

Table 4-4   DOS/Windows A+ Objectives

Objectives	Chapters	Page Numbers
2.2 Identify typical memory conflict problems and how to optimize memory use.	4, 12	
A. What a memory conflict is	12	620-622
B. How it happens	12	620-622
C. When to employ utilities	12	620-622
E. General Protection Fault	12	620-622
F. Illegal operations occurrences	12	620-622
G. MemMaker or other optimization utilities	4	207, 208
H. Himem.sys	4	204

Review Questions

Circle True or False.

1. Windows 9x has the ability to manage its own swap file.   **True / False**

2. If you have a new computer, it is always recommended that you disable your virtual memory because it isn't needed.   **True / False**

3. Changing the virtual memory setting in Windows 9x has the same effect as changing the swap file size in Windows 3.x.   **True / False**

4. In Windows 9x each program has its own swap file.   **True / False**

5. How many swap files can Windows 9x use at the same time?

   _____

6. You are employed as a desktop PC support technician at the Sweet Town hot water company. Billy, one of your customers, has asked that you show him how to disable the swap file setting on his laptop. In the space below, write the instructions for Billy to modify the memory configuration of his laptop.

   _____

   _____

   _____

   _____

   _____

LAB 4.4 MEMORY MANAGEMENT IN WINDOWS NT

Objective

The objective of this lab exercise is to teach you how to manage and control memory allocations in the Windows NT environment. After completing this lab exercise, you will be able to:

- Properly configure one or multiple Windows NT swap files.
- Describe the optimum virtual memory configuration for the Windows NT operating system.
- Configure the maximum registry size.

Materials Required

This lab exercise requires one complete lab workstation for every four students. The lab workstation should meet the following requirements:

- 486 or better
- 16MB of RAM
- Windows NT

Lab Setup & Safety Tips

- Each lab workstation should have Windows NT Workstation installed and functioning properly.
- Each lab workstation must be configured with a D partition.

ACTIVITY

Configuring the Windows NT swap file

1. Right-click the **My Computer** icon, and then click **Properties**.
2. Click the **Performance** tab.
3. Click the **Change** button.
4. Click in the **Initial Size** box and set the value to **85**.
5. Click in the **Maximum Size** box and set the value to **100**.
6. Click the **Set** button.
7. Click the **OK** button.
8. Click the **Close** button.
9. Click the **Yes** button to restart your lab workstation.

Configuring multiple swap files

1. Right-click the **My Computer** icon, and then click **Properties**.
2. Click the **Performance** tab.
3. Click the **Change** button.
4. At the top of the virtual memory property sheet, select drive **D**.
5. Click in the **Initial Size** box and set the value to **85**.
6. Click in the **Maximum Size** box and set the value to **100**.
7. Click the **Set** button.

8. Click the **OK** button.

9. Click the **Close** button.

10. Click the **Yes** button to restart your lab workstation.

Controlling the Windows NT registry size

1. Right-click the **My Computer** icon, and then click **Properties**.

2. Click the **Performance** tab.

3. Click the **Change** button.

4. Click in the **Maximum Registry Size** box and set the value to **10**.

5. Click the **OK** button.

6. Click the **Close** button.

7. Click the **Yes** button to restart your lab workstation.

Lab Notes

What are the ideal virtual memory settings for Windows NT?—To obtain optimum performance from the Windows NT operating system, Microsoft recommends that you place one swap file on each physical hard drive except the hard drive that contains the Windows NT system directory.

What is the ideal registry size?—For most Windows NT installations it isn't necessary to modify the registry size parameter. Should it become necessary to adjust the maximum registry size parameter on a Windows NT Workstation, don't allow it to grow larger than 14MB.

Review Questions

Circle True or False.

1. Windows NT supports the use of multiple swap files at the same time.   True / False

2. When working in the Windows NT environment, it is recommended that you maintain a 20MB swap file at all times.   True / False

3. The largest swap file Windows NT workstation supports is 40MB.   True / False

4. In Windows NT you can control the maximum size of the registry.   True / False

5. Describe how to configure Windows NT Workstation to use multiple swap files.

_____

_____

_____

_____

_____

6. Jimmy just installed Windows NT workstation on his PC. He has asked you to explain how he can move his swap file from his drive C to his drive D. In the space below, write the instructions you would give to Jimmy.

_____

_____

_____

_____

5

FLOPPY DRIVES AND OTHER ESSENTIAL DEVICES

LABS INCLUDED IN THIS CHAPTER

♦ LAB 5.1 CONFIGURING A SINGLE FLOPPY DRIVE

♦ LAB 5.2 CONFIGURING A DUAL FLOPPY DRIVE SYSTEM

LAB 5.1 CONFIGURING A SINGLE FLOPPY DRIVE

Objective

The objective of this lab is to provide you with the hands-on experience of removing, installing, and configuring a floppy drive. After completing this lab exercise, you will be able to:

- Install a single floppy disk drive in a PC.

- Configure a single floppy disk drive to function properly within a PC system.

- Remove a single floppy disk drive from a PC.

Materials Required

One Windows 9x lab workstation for every four students. The lab workstations should meet the following requirements:

- 486 or better

- At least 16MB of RAM

- 540MB or larger hard drive

Necessary data cable and controller to allow for a 5.25-inch floppy drive installation

One ESD mat for each lab workstation

One grounding strap for each student

One 3.5-inch floppy drive installed in each lab workstation

One 5.25-inch floppy drive for each lab workstation

One 5.25-floppy disk

Necessary tools to remove the case and to mount/dismount-inch floppy drives

Lab Setup & Safety Tips

- Each lab workstation should have Window 9x installed and functioning properly.

- Each lab workstation should have one 3.5-inch floppy drive installed and functioning properly.

- Each lab workstation should have one available 5.25-inch bay.

- Each group of students should be given one 5.25-inch floppy drive.

- Students must comply with standard ESD procedures.

- Always unplug the power cord before touching any component within the case.

ACTIVITY

Removing the 3.5-inch floppy drive

1. Power off your PC.

2. Verify that you are properly grounded.

3. Unplug the power cord from the system unit.

4. Remove the top of the case.

5. Unplug the data cable connected to the 3.5-inch floppy drive.

6. Unplug the power connector for the 3.5-inch floppy drive.

7. Dismount the 3.5-inch floppy drive.

8. Remove the 3.5-inch floppy drive from your lab workstation.

9. Stand clear of the case and plug in the power cord.

10. Power on your lab workstation, and enter the CMOS Setup program.

11. Remove the 3.5-inch floppy drive from the Setup program.

12. Save your changes and reboot your lab workstation.

Removing the 3.5-inch floppy drive from Windows

1. Allow your lab workstation to boot into Windows 9x.

2. Double-click the **My Computer** icon.

3. Verify that Windows 9x does not recognize any floppy drives.

4. If there still is an icon for the 3.5-inch floppy drive, complete the following steps:

   a. Click the **Start** button.

   b. Point to **Settings** and click **Control Panel**.

   c. Double-click the **System** icon.

   d. Click the **Device Manager** tab.

   e. Double-click the **Floppy disk controllers** icon.

   f. Click the **3.5 floppy drive** icon to highlight it.

   g. Press **Delete**.

   h. Click the **Yes** button on the confirmation message.

   i. Reboot your lab workstation, then double-click the **My Computer** icon to verify that Windows doesn't recognize any floppy drives.

Installing a 5.25-inch floppy drive

1. Power off your PC.

2. Verify that you are properly grounded.

3. Unplug the power cord from the system unit.

4. Remove the top of the case.

5. Locate an available 5.25-inch drive bay.

6. Remove any blanks that may be in place.

7. Slide the 5.25-inch floppy drive into the bay.

8. Plug in the data cable.

9. Plug in the power connector.

10. Stand clear of the case and plug in the power cord.

11. Power on your lab workstation.

12. Enter the CMOS Setup program.

13. Configure the Setup program to recognize the 5.25-inch floppy drive.

14. Save the CMOS settings and reboot your lab workstation.

Testing the 5.25-inch floppy drive

1. Allow your lab workstation to boot into Windows 9x.

2. Double-click the **My Computer** icon.

3. Verify that Windows 9x recognizes the 5.25 floppy drive.

4. Insert the 5.25-inch floppy disk into the 5.25-inch floppy drive.

5. Right-click the **5.25 floppy drive** icon, and select **Format**.

6. Click the **Start** button in the Format dialog box.

7. When the formatting is complete, click the **Close** button.

8. In the Format dialog box, click the **Close** button.

9. Close the My Computer window.

If Windows 9x does not detect the floppy drive

1. Click the **Start** button.

2. Point to **Settings** and click **Control Panel**.

3. Double-click the **Add New Hardware** icon.

4. Click the **Next** button three times to allow Windows to detect new hardware.

5. When the process is complete, allow Windows to install the proper device driver.

6. Reboot your lab workstation, and follow the steps in the section, "Testing the 5.25-inch floppy drive."

Lab Notes

How do I know which way to connect a data cable?—All PC data cables have a red stripe along one side of the cable. This stripe should always be aligned with the number one pin on the attached device. The stripe is sometimes blue.

What is BOOT PRIORITY?—Boot priority is a value assigned to a bootable device that communicates to a computer the order in which it should attempt to boot from a bootable device. For example, if a floppy drive is assigned a boot priority of 1, and a hard drive in the same computer is assigned a boot priority of 2, the computer will attempt to boot from the floppy drive before the hard drive. Note that the boot priority is also known as the boot sequence and can normally be customized by using the CMOS Setup program.

Why does my computer boot from the CD-ROM?—Because CD-ROMs are becoming more common, some CD-ROM drives are now boot capable. This means that a boot-capable CD-ROM drive can be assigned a boot priority just like a floppy drive or a hard drive.

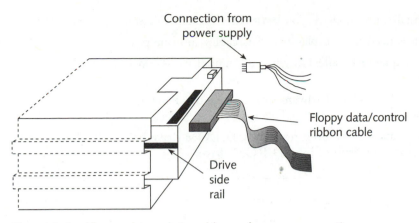

Figure 5-1   Floppy drive, data cable, and power connection

A+ ## CERTIFICATION OBJECTIVES

Table 5-1   Core A+ Objectives

Objectives	Chapters	Page Numbers
4.4 Identify the purpose of CMOS (Complementary Metal-Oxide Semiconductor), what it contains and how to change its basic parameters.	3, 9, Appendix B	
3. Floppy drive	3	159, 160
a. enable/disable drive or boot	3	159, 160
b. speed	3	139, 160
c. density	3	159, 160
6. Boot sequence	3	159, 160

Table 5-2   DOS/Windows A+ Objectives

Objectives	Chapters	Page Numbers
3.4 Identify procedures for loading/adding device drivers and the necessary software for certain devices.	4, 9, 10	
A. Windows 3.x procedures	4	198, 199
B. Windows 95 Plug and Play	9, 10	459-461, 526

1. When you install a floppy drive, you must enter the CMOS Setup program.   True / False

2. All floppy drives need three cables: two data cables and one power connector.   True / False

3. Can the boot sequence be affected when a floppy drive is added or removed from a PC?
True / False

4. You can use the Add New Hardware icon on Control Panel to allow Windows to automatically detect new hardware.   True / False

5. John's computer attempts to boot from his CD-ROM drive before the floppy drive. How can he change the boot priority of his CD-ROM drive?

_____

_____

_____

_____

_____

6. What must you do after physically installing a floppy drive?

_____

_____

_____

_____

7. Stacey just installed a floppy drive into her PC, but the floppy drive icon does not show up when she boots into Windows. Assuming that she installed the drive correctly, what would you recommend Stacey do to make Windows recognize her new floppy drive?

_____

_____

_____

_____

_____

LAB 5.2 CONFIGURING A DUAL FLOPPY DRIVE SYSTEM

Objective

The objective of this lab is to provide you with the hands-on skills necessary to configure dual floppy drives on a personal computer. After completing this lab exercise you will be able to:

- Install dual floppy disk drives in a personal computer.

- Properly configure a personal computer to use two floppy disk drives.

Materials Required

One Windows 9x lab workstation for every four students. The lab workstations should meet the following requirements:

- 486 or better

- At least 16MB of RAM

- 540MB or larger hard drive

Necessary data cables and controllers to allow for a 5.25-inch and a 3.5-inch floppy drive installation

One ESD mat for each lab workstation

One grounding strap for each student

One 3.5-inch inch floppy drive for each lab workstation

One 5.25-inch floppy disk

One 3.5-inch floppy disk

Necessary tools to remove the case and to mount/dismount floppy drives

Lab Setup & Safety Tips

- Each lab workstation should have Window 9x installed and functioning properly.

- Each lab workstation should have one 5.25-inch floppy drive installed and functioning properly.

- Each lab workstation should have one available 3.5-inch bay.

- Each group of students should be given one 3.5-inch floppy drive.

- Students must comply with standard ESD procedures.

- Always unplug the power cord before touching any component within the case.

ACTIVITY

Installing a 3.5-inch floppy drive as drive A

1. Power off your PC.

2. Verify that you are properly grounded.

3. Unplug the power cord from the system unit.

4. Remove the top of the case.

5. Locate an available 3.5-inch drive bay.

6. Remove any blanks that may be in place.

7. Slide the 3.5-inch floppy drive into the bay.

8. Plug in the data cable.

9. Plug in the power connector.

10. Stand clear of the case and plug in the power cord.

11. Power on your lab workstation.

12. Enter the CMOS Setup program.

13. Configure the Setup program to recognize the 3.5-inch floppy drive.

14. Save the CMOS settings and reboot your lab workstation.

Testing the 3.5-inch floppy drive

1. Allow your lab workstation to boot into Windows 9x.

2. Double-click the **My Computer** icon.

3. Verify that Windows 9x recognizes the 3.5-inch floppy drive.

4. Insert the 3.5-inch floppy disk into the 3.5-inch floppy drive.

5. Right-click the **3.5 floppy drive** icon and select **Format**.

6. Click the **Start** button in the Format dialog box.

7. When the formatting is complete, click the **Close** button.

8. In the Format dialog box, click the **Close** button.

9. Close the My Computer window.

Testing the 5.25-inch floppy drive as drive B

1. Allow your lab workstation to boot into Windows 9x.

2. Double-click the **My Computer** icon.

3. Verify that Windows 9x recognizes the 5.25-inch floppy drive.

4. Insert the 5.25-inch floppy disk into the 5.25-inch floppy drive.

5. Right-click the **5.25 floppy drive** icon, and select **Format**.

6. Click the **Start** button in the Format dialog box.

7. When the formatting is complete, click the **Close** button.

8. In the Format dialog box, click the **Close** button.

9. Close the My Computer window.

If Windows 9x does not detect the floppy drive

1. Click the **Start** button.

2. Point to **Settings** and click **Control Panel**.

3. Double-click the **Add New Hardware** icon.

4. Click the **Next** button three times to allow Windows to detect the new hardware.

5. When the process is complete, allow Windows to install the proper device driver.

6. Reboot your lab workstation, and follow the steps in the section, "Testing the 3.5-inch floppy drive."

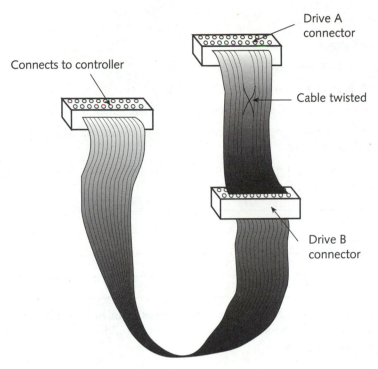

Figure 5-2   Twist in the cable

> **Lab Notes**
>
> **How do I configure two floppy drives using the same data cable?**—Figure 5-2 above shows an example of a typical floppy drive cable that could be used to configure multiple drives. Note that the twist in the data cable helps the computer differentiate between floppy drives A and B.

A+ CERTIFICATION OBJECTIVES

Table 5-3   Core A+ Objectives

Objectives	Chapters	Page Numbers
4.4 Identify the purpose of CMOS (Complementary Metal-Oxide Semiconductor), what it contains, and how to change its basic parameters.	3, 6, Appendix B	
3. Floppy drive	3	159, 160
a. enable/disable drive or boot	3	159, 160
b. speed	3	159, 160
c. density	3	159, 160
6. Boot sequence	3	159, 160

Table 5-4   DOS/Windows A+ Objectives

Objectives	Chapters	Page Numbers
3.4 Identify procedures for loading/adding device drivers and the necessary software for certain devices.	4, 9, 10	
A. Windows 3.x procedures	4	198, 199
B. Windows 95 Plug and Play	9, 10	459-461, 526

Review Questions

Circle True or False.

1. PCs always boot to drive B first. True / False

2. Your drive A is always a hard drive. True / False

3. A PC can have only two floppy drives. True / False

4. A 3.5-inch high-density floppy disk typically holds more data than a 5.25-inch high-density floppy disk. True / False

5. Alice, who uses Windows 9x, wants to know how to format a 3.5-inch floppy disk. List the steps below.

   _____

   _____

   _____

   _____

   _____

6. Dave has recently removed one of his floppy drives from his PC. He now receives an error message every time he reboots his computer. What would you recommend Dave do to eliminate this error message?

   _____

   _____

   _____

   _____

   _____

6

INTRODUCTION TO HARD DRIVES

LABS INCLUDED IN THIS CHAPTER

♦ **LAB 6.1** HARD DRIVE MANAGEMENT

♦ **LAB 6.2** HARD DRIVE PREPARATION AND OPTIMIZATION

♦ **LAB 6.3** HARD DRIVE ORGANIZATION

♦ **LAB 6.4** REMOVABLE DRIVE CONFIGURATION

LAB 6.1 HARD DRIVE MANAGEMENT

Objective

The FDISK utility allows you to add, remove, and view your hard drive's partition configuration. After completing this lab exercise, you will be able to:

- Use the FDISK utility to view drive configuration information.
- Add and remove partitions using the FDISK utility.
- Use the FDISK utility to set an active partition.
- Describe the relationship between a logical drive and an extended partition.

Materials Required

This lab exercise requires one complete lab workstation for every four students. The lab workstation should meet the following requirements:

- 486 or better
- 16MB of RAM
- Windows 9x
- 540MB hard drive

The DOS system disk created in Lab 1.2

Lab Setup & Safety Tips

- Each workstation's hard drive should contain at least one partition.
- *Warning*: The steps in the following Activity will erase all data currently stored on your lab workstation. Back up any stored data before proceeding.
- Any changes made using the FDISK utility will affect the data stored on the partition or partitions that were modified. *Be careful!*

ACTIVITY

Viewing the current hard drive configuration

1. Power off your lab workstation
2. Insert the boot disk into drive A.
3. Power on your lab workstation and allow it to boot from the floppy disk.
4. At the A prompt, type **FDISK**.
5. From the FDISK menu, select option 4 by typing **4** and pressing **Enter**.
6. Observe your current hard drive configuration.

Deleting a partition

1. Press the **Esc** key to return to the Main Menu.
2. From the FDISK Main Menu, select option 3 by typing **3** and pressing **Enter**.
3. Select the primary partition on your hard drive by typing **1** and pressing **Enter**.
4. Type **1** and press **Enter**.
5. Type the volume label of the primary partition.

6. Confirm the deletion by typing **Y** and pressing **Enter**.

7. Press the **Esc** key to return to the Main Menu.

8. Press **Esc** again to exit the FDISK utility.

9. Press the **spacebar** to restart the computer and the workstation.

Creating a partition

1. Boot the workstation using the floppy disk.

2. At the A prompt, type **FDISK**.

3. At the FDISK Main Menu, select option **1** and press **Enter**.

4. Type **1** and press **Enter**.

5. When the FDISK utility asks if you would like to use all of the available space for the primary partition and set it active, select No by typing **N** and pressing **Enter**.

6. When FDISK prompts you to enter the amount of drive space you would like to use, type **500** and press **Enter**.

7. If prompted for a volume label, type **DRIVE 1** and press **Enter**.

8. Press **Esc** to return to the FDISK Main Menu.

Setting an active partition

1. Select option **2** from the FDISK Main Menu.

2. Choose the primary partition that you created by typing **1** and pressing **Enter**.

3. Press **Esc** to return to the main menu.

4. Press **Esc** to exit FDISK and press any key. Your workstation will restart.

Lab Notes

Extended partition—An extended partition is a section of the hard drive that allows the partitioning of logical drives. Note that there can be only one extended partition per hard drive.

Logical drive—A logical drive is a partition that holds a drive letter and behaves as a separate physical drive. Note that logical drives can be created only within extended partitions.

Active partition—If a partition is set as active, the system will attempt to boot from that partition.

FDISK/MBR—This command is used to refresh the master boot record without causing any data loss.

A+ | **CERTIFICATION OBJECTIVES**

Table 6-1   DOS/Windows A+ Objectives

Objectives	Chapters	Page Numbers
1.4 Identify the procedures for basic disk management.	5, 6, 7, 18, Appendix F	
A. Using disk management utilities	6	320-322
C. Formatting	5, 6, 7	246, 283, 294, 361
D. Partitioning	6, 7	294-297, 359-361
3.1 Identify the procedures for installing DOS, Windows 3.x, and Windows 95, and for bringing the software to a basic operational level.	6, 7, 12	
A. Partition	6, 7	294-297, 359-361
4.3 Recognize common problems and determine how to resolve them.	1, 4, 5, 8, 12, 16	
B. DOS and Windows-based utilities		
7. Fdisk.exe	8	411

Review Questions

Circle True or False.

1. When a partition's size is changed using the FDISK utility, the data contained on the partition is lost. True / False

2. The FDISK utility is used to partition and format hard drives. True / False

3. The FDISK utility refers to hard drive capacity in bytes. True / False

4. Extended partitions are always placed with logical drives. True / False

5. List three functions of the FDISK utility.

_____

_____

_____

6. What will happen if an active partition is not set?

_____

_____

7. You are the desktop PC support technician for the Good Job Corporation. John, one of your customers, suspects that his hard drive is not partitioned to use its full capacity. Describe how you would use the FDISK utility to show John his current hard drive configuration.

_____

_____

_____

8. Describe the relationship between a logical drive and an extended partition.

_____

_____

_____

LAB 6.2 HARD DRIVE PREPARATION AND OPTIMIZATION

Objective

Formatting a hard drive is the procedure used to install a file system onto a newly partitioned hard drive. In this lab exercise you will learn how to properly install and optimize the FAT file system. After completing this lab exercise, you will be able to:

- Format a partition.
- Use and then describe how the SCANDISK utility can be used to optimize drive performance.
- Use and then describe how the DEFRAG utility can be used to optimize drive performance.

Materials Required

This lab exercise requires a minimum of one complete lab workstation for each student.

- 486 or better
- 16MB of RAM
- 540MB hard drive

One DOS boot disk that includes the Format and SYS commands.

One DOS disk that contains both the SCANDISK and DEFRAG utilities.

Lab Setup & Safety Tips

- Each workstation's hard drive should contain one unformatted primary partition that has been set as active.
- Be sure that the data stored on your lab workstation has been backed up before proceeding with this lab exercise.

ACTIVITY

Formatting the C drive

1. Power off your lab workstation.
2. Insert the boot disk into drive A.
3. Power on your lab workstation and allow it to boot from your DOS boot disk.
4. At the A prompt, type **FORMAT C:**.
5. When asked to confirm before proceeding, type **Y** and press **Enter**. The format command will begin to format drive C.
6. When formatting is complete, type a volume label of **DRIVE 1**.

Making drive C bootable

You can use many different commands to make a drive bootable. Following are two examples of command sequences:

Example 1

1. Power off your lab workstation.
2. Insert the boot disk into drive A.

3. Power on your lab workstation and allow it to boot from your DOS boot disk.

4. At the A prompt, type **SYS A: C:** and press **Enter**.

Example 2

The /S switch tells DOS to add system information to the drive after it has been formatted. Use the /? option to view other FORMAT switches.

1. Power off your lab workstation.

2. Insert the boot disk into drive A.

3. Power on your lab workstation and allow it to boot from your DOS boot disk.

4. At the A prompt, type **FORMAT C: /S**.

5. When asked to confirm before proceeding, type **Y** and press **Enter**.

6. When formatting is complete, type in a volume label of **DRIVE 1**.

Using the SCANDISK utility

1. Insert the disk that contains the SCANDISK utility.

2. At the A prompt, type **SCANDISK** and press **Enter**.

3. Allow SCANDISK to verify your file and directory structure, and to complete a surface scan.

4. When SCANDISK has completed, use the **View Log** option to view any errors that SCANDISK might have encountered.

5. After examining the view log, exit the SCANDISK utility.

Using the DEFRAG utility

1. Insert the disk that contains the DEFRAG utility.

2. At the A prompt, type **DEFRAG** and press **Enter**.

3. Allow DEFRAG to reorganize the hard drive (this should happen quickly if the drive was formatted recently).

4. When the defragmentation is complete, exit the DEFRAG utility.

 Lab Notes

What is a switch?—A switch is a parameter or variable that can be added to the end of a DOS command and which will change or enhance the meaning of the command.

DEFRAG—This utility is designed to optimize file access by moving file clusters into a continuous chain, thus speeding up data retrieval. This utility should be used at least once a month to maintain optimum performance.

SCANDISK—This utility is designed to search a hard drive for lost or cross-linked clusters and attempt to repair them. SCANDISK should be used at least once a month to maintain optimum performance. Note that regular use of the SCANDISK and DEFRAG utilities can improve system performance.

CERTIFICATION OBJECTIVES

Table 6-2   DOS/Windows A+ Objectives

Objectives	Chapters	Page Numbers
1.4 Identify the procedures for basic disk management.	5, 6, 7, 18, Appendix F	
A. Using disk management utilities	6	320-322
E. Defragmenting	6	320-322
F. ScanDisk	6	322
3.1 Identify the procedures for installing DOS, Windows 3.x, and Windows 95, and for bringing the software to a basic operational level.	6, 7, 12	
B. Format drive	6, 7	294, 359-361
4.3 Recognize common problems and determine how to resolve them.	1, 4, 5, 8, 12, 16	
B. DOS and Windows-based utilities		
1. ScanDisk	8	411
5. Defrag.exe	8	411

6

Review Questions

Circle True or False.

1. Using the SCANDISK utility will delete all files less than 512 K in size. True / False

2. The DEFRAG utility places file clusters in consecutive order. True / False

3. You should run the SCANDISK utility only once every three months. True / False

4. Newly created partitions always need to be formatted before you install an operating system. True / False

5. Describe the functionality of the DEFRAG utility.

_____

_____

_____

_____

_____

6. You are currently employed as a PC desktop support technician at the Our World Corporation. One of your customers, Jamie, calls to tell you that her computer is running more slowly than it did last month. List two things that might help improve the performance of Jamie's computer.

_____

_____

_____

_____

_____

7. John is currently running DEFRAG, and it is taking a long time. John calls you to ask what the DEFRAG program is doing and why it seems to be so slow. Note that over the last year John has never run the DEFRAG utility. Describe to John both the purpose of the DEFRAG utility and explain why it is taking so long to run.

_____

_____

_____

_____

_____

LAB 6.3 HARD DRIVE ORGANIZATION

Objective

The objective of this lab exercise is to provide you with the installation, configuration, and navigation experience necessary to control the DOS environment. After completing this lab exercise, you will be able to:

- Navigate the DOS directory structure.
- Identify DOS system files.
- Explain DOS file naming conventions, and rename both files and directories.
- Manipulate file attributes in the DOS environment.

Materials Required

This lab exercise requires one lab workstation for every four students. The lab workstation should meet the following requirements:

- 486 or better
- 16MB of RAM
- One formatted 540MB or larger hard drive
- DOS 5.0 or higher

Lab Setup & Safety Tips

- Each lab workstation should have DOS 5.0, or later, installed and functioning properly.

ACTIVITY

Navigating the DOS environment

1. To briefly observe the DOS directory structure, type **TREE C:** at the C prompt and press **Enter**. The result will be a diagram of the current directory structure of your hard drive.

2. Boot your lab workstation to the C prompt.

3. To create a directory named Student, type **MD STUDENT** and press **Enter**.

4. Observe where the Student directory is now located in the DOS directory structure. Type **TREE c:** and press **Enter**.

5. To change to the Student directory, type **CD STUDENT** and press **Enter**.

6. To copy the Config.sys file to the Student directory, type **COPY C:\CONFIG.SYS C:\STUDENT** and press **Enter**.

7. To view the contents of the Student directory, type **DIR** and press **Enter**.

8. Observe that the Config.sys file is now in the Student directory.

Renaming a file

1. To rename the Config.sys in the Student directory, type **REN C:\STUDENT\CONFIG.SYS CONFIG.OLD**.

2. To observe the results, type **DIR** and press **Enter**.

Renaming a directory

1. Type **CD ** and press **Enter**.

2. To rename the Student directory to Student2, type **MOVE C:\STUDENT C:\STUDENT2** and press **Enter**.

3. To observe the results, type **DIR** and press **Enter**.

Viewing and changing file attributes

1. To change to the Student2 directory, type **CD STUDENT2** and press **Enter**.

2. To view the attributes of the config.old, type **ATTRIB C:\STUDENT2\ CONFIG.OLD** and press **Enter**.

3. To make the config.old file a hidden file, type **ATTRIB +H C:\STUDENT2\CONFIG.OLD** and press **Enter**.

4. To observe the results, type **DIR** and press **Enter**.

5. To remove the hidden attribute from the config.old file, type **ATTRIB –H C:\STUDENT2\CONFIG.OLD** and press **Enter**.

Editing DOS configuration files

1. Type **EDIT** at the C prompt and press **Enter**.

2. Press the **Alt** key to highlight the File option in the upper-left corner of the Edit program.

3. Press the down arrow [↓] to select the **Open** option from the File menu.

4. Press **Enter**.

5. In the Open dialog box, type **C:\STUDENT2\CONFIG.OLD** and press **Enter**.

6. Press the **Alt** key to highlight the File option in the upper-left corner of the Edit program.

7. Use the down arrow [↓] to select the **Exit** option from the File menu.

8. Press **Enter**.

Lab Notes

ATTRIB +/– H—These commands set the Hidden file attribute.

ATTRIB +/– A—These commands set the Archive file attribute.

ATTRIB +/– R—These commands set the Read file attribute.

ATTRIB +/– S—These commands set the System file attribute.

The following is a list of the files used to initialize the DOS operating system.

- MSDOS.SYS
- COMMAND.COM
- IO.SYS

The following are both text files stored in the root directory and are used to customize the DOS environment.

- AUTOEXEC.BAT
- CONFIG.SYS

DOS error messages

Incorrect DOS version—This error most commonly occurs when you try to execute a newer DOS command from an older version of DOS.

Error in CONFIG.SYS line xx—You see this error message during the boot process if there is an error in the CONFIG.SYS file. The xx will be the line number starting from the top of the file and counting down.

Invalid or missing COMMAND.COM—This error message appears when COMMAND.COM is not present, is corrupt, or is the wrong version.

Remember that the DOS file naming convention includes an eight-character filename and a three-character file extension that is separated by a period.

CERTIFICATION OBJECTIVES

Table 6-3   DOS/Windows A+ Objectives

Objectives	Chapters	Page Numbers
1.1 Identify the operating system's functions, structure,. and major system files	1, 2, 4, 12, Appendices C and E	
B. Major components of DOS, Windows 3.x and Windows 95.	1, 2	35, 74
C. Contrasts between Windows 3.x and Windows 95.	1, 2	35, 75, 76
D. Major system files: what they are, where they are located, how they are used and what they contain:	2, 4, 12	74-77, 188, 198-200, 598-600
1. System, Configuration, and User Interface files	2, 4, 12	74-77, 188, 198-200, 598-600
A. DOS		
1. Autoexec.bat	2, 4	75, 76, 198, 199
2. Config.sys	2, 4	75, 198, 199
3. Io.sys	2	74
4. Ansi.sys	Appendix C	C1-C4
5. Msdos.sys	2	74
7. HIMEM.SYS	4	188, 198, 199
8. Command.com (internal DOS commands)	2, 4	75
C. Windows 95		
1. Io.sys	2	74
2. Msdos.sys	2	75
3. Command.com	2	74
1.2 Identify ways to navigate the operating system and how to get to needed technical information.	1, 12	
A. Procedures (e.g., menu or icon –driven) for navigating through DOS to perform such things as locating, accessing, and retrieving information.	1	44
1.3 Identify basic concepts and procedures for creating, viewing and managing files and directories, including procedures for changing file attributes and the ramifications of those changes (for example, security issues).	1, 6	
A. File attributes	6	313-319
B. File naming conventions	1	40
C. Command syntax	6	310-314
D. Read Only, Hidden, System, and Archive attributes	6	313-319
3.1 Identify the procedures for installing DOS, Windows 3.x, and Windows 95, and for bringing the software to a basic operational level.	6, 7, 12	
C. Run appropriate set up utility	7, 12	362, 637, 638
4.1 Recognize and interpret the meaning of common error codes and startup messages from the boot sequence, and identify steps to correct the problems.	4, 5, 7, 8, 12	
B. Incorrect DOS version	5, Appendix A	266, A2
D. Error in CONFIG.SYS line XX	12	603

6

Table 6-3   DOS/Windows A+ Objectives (continued)

Objectives	Chapters	Page Numbers
4.3 Recognize common problems and determine how to . resolve them	1, 4, 5, 8, 12, 16	
B. DOS and Windows-based utilities		
3. ATTRIB.EXE	8	411
6. Edit.com	8	411

Review Questions

Circle True or False.

1. You can rename a directory by using the REN command. **True / False**

2. When you receive the error message "Invalid or missing command.com" it means that the entire operating system is corrupt and must be reinstalled. **True / False**

3. What does the CD command stand for?

_____

_____

_____

_____

_____

4. What is the ATTRIB command used for?

_____

_____

_____

_____

_____

5. Name one required DOS system file.

_____

_____

_____

_____

6. Patrick, one of your customers, is trying to find a file that is located in the MyData directory on his computer. What command would you suggest that Patrick use to view the contents of the MyData directory?

_____

_____

_____

_____

7. List the three DOS system files that are used during startup.

_____

_____

_____

_____

_____

8. John is attempting to rename his c:\Mydata directory to c:\stuff, but his computer won't let him. Describe the steps John needs to take to rename the c:\Mdata directory to c:\stuff.

_____

_____

_____

_____

_____

6

LAB 6.4 REMOVABLE DRIVE CONFIGURATION

Objective

The objective of this lab exercise is to enable you to install a removable drive. After completing this lab exercise, you will be able to:

- Install an external removable drive.

- Name several types of removable drive technology.

Materials Required

This lab exercise requires one complete lab workstation for each group of four students. The lab workstation should meet the following requirements:

- 486 or better

- 16MB of RAM

- 540MB or larger hard drive

- Windows 9x

One removable (Zip or similar) tape drive for each group of four students

Lab Setup & Safety Tips

- To ensure complete data safety, *never* install or remove a removable drive while the PC is powered on.

- Each lab workstation should have Windows 9x installed and functioning properly.

- The parallel port should be configured for use.

ACTIVITY

Adding a removable drive

1. Power off your lab workstation.

2. Connect the lab workstation's external drive to the parallel port.

3. Verify that the external drive is plugged in.

4. Power on the lab workstation and allow it to boot into Windows 9X.

5. Insert the driver disk for the external drive.

6. Follow the instructions for installing the drivers, or ask your instructor for details.

7. After the drivers are installed, reboot the lab workstation.

8. Test your drive installation by typing **CD** and the drive letter of the removable drive (for example, **CD d**).

Lab Notes

Depending on the type of removable drive, the driver installation steps will vary. The following is a list of some commonly used external removable drives:

Iomega Zip drives

Iomega Jaz drives

Tape backup drives

SyJet drives

Magneto-optical drives

Phase-dual (PD) optical drives

CD-R (writeable CD-ROM drive)

CD-RW (Rewriteable CD-ROM drive)

6

A+ | CERTIFICATION OBJECTIVES

Table 6-4   Core A+ Objectives

Objectives	Chapters	Page Numbers
1.2 Identify basic procedures for adding and removing field replaceable modules.	1, 2, 11, 15	
B. Storage device	1, 14	11, 774-779
1.7 Identify proper procedures for installing and configuring peripheral devices.	14, 15	
C. Storage devices	14	781-782

Review Questions

Circle True or False.

1. Drivers for external drives are always sold separately. True / False

2. External drives are always attached by way of a parallel port. True / False

3. Windows 9x will always automatically detect an external drive. True / False

4. Name two types of external drives.

_____

_____

_____

_____

5. List several reasons you would use an external removable drive.

_____

_____

_____

_____

_____

6. You are employed at the COMP Computer Outlet as a service technician. Bobby, one of your favorite customers, has just bought a new Zip drive and is trying to configure it. He explains to you that he is using Windows 9x and has attached his Zip drive to the proper port, but Windows still will not detect his Zip drive. List the first three questions you would ask Bobby to help discover the problem.

_____

_____

_____

_____

_____

Hard Drive Installation and Support

LABS INCLUDED IN THIS CHAPTER

♦ **Lab 7.1 Configuring a Single Hard Drive System**

♦ **Lab 7.2 Configuring a Dual Hard Drive System**

LAB 7.1 CONFIGURING A SINGLE HARD DRIVE SYSTEM

Objective

The objective of this lab exercise is to configure one IDE hard drive when a slave is not present. After completing this lab exercise, you will be able to:

- Install and remove an IDE hard drive.

Materials Required

This lab exercise requires a minimum of one lab workstation for every two students. Each workstation should meet the following requirements:

- 486 or better
- 16MB of RAM
- One 540MB or larger IDE hard drive

One Torx bit driver and any other tools necessary to open each lab workstation's case

Lab Setup & Safety Tips

- Each student must be properly grounded using a grounding mat and grounding strap. If students are working in pairs, identify one as Student 1 and the other as Student 2.
- Students must comply with standard ESD procedures.
- Always unplug the power cord before touching any component within the case.

ACTIVITY

Removing an IDE hard drive

Student 1

1. Power off the lab workstation and unplug the power cord (it is not necessary to unplug all other cords).
2. Remove the case from the lab workstation.
3. Locate the hard drive.
4. Unplug the IDE cable and the power connector from the hard drive. Note the position of the data and power connector.
5. Use the Torx bit driver or a screwdriver to dismount the hard drive.
6. Stand clear of the workstation and plug in the power cord.
7. With the hard drive removed, power on the lab workstation and wait for the BIOS error message.
8. Enter the Setup program, if necessary, and follow the menu instructions for the workstation's BIOS to validate the hard drive changes.
9. Save the changes and reboot the workstation.

Installing an IDE hard drive

Student 2

1. Power off the lab workstation and unplug the power cord.
2. Using the hard drive taken from Student 1's CPU, mount the hard drive in its original position.

3. Connect the IDE data cable and the power connector. (Be sure that you connect the cables in the same manner they were previously connected. The red stripe on the data cable should be aligned with the pin 1 setting on the hard drive).

4. Stand clear of the workstation and plug in the power cord.

5. When the workstation boots, enter the Setup program.

6. Verify that the BIOS has automatically detected the hard drive.

7. Save the BIOS changes and exit the Setup program.

8. Reboot the workstation and test the installation by booting into the operating system.

9. Shut down the workstation and power it off.

10. Unplug the power cable and secure the case.

11. Plug the workstation back in and power it on.

> **TIP**
>
> ## Lab Notes
>
> Remember that the red stripe on an IDE data cable should always be aligned with the pin 1 on the device to which it is being connected. (*Note:* When you are connecting an IDE hard drive to an IDE data cable, the red stripe or pin on one side should be attached to the same side of the hard drive as the power connector.)

CERTIFICATION OBJECTIVES

Table 7-1 Core A+ Objectives

Objectives	Chapters	Page Numbers
1.2 Identify basic procedures for adding and removing field replaceable modules.	1, 3, 4, 11, 14	
B. Storage device	1, 14	11, 774-779
1.5 Identify proper procedures for installing and configuring IDE/EIDE devices.	6, 7	
A. Master/Slave	6, 7	282, 348-354
B. Devices per channel	6, 7	282, 348-354
1.7 Identify proper procedures for installing and configuring peripheral devices.	14, 15	
C. Storage devices	14	781, 782
2.1 Identify common symptoms and problems associated with each module and how to troubleshoot and isolate the problems.	2, 3, 5, 7, 8 10, 11, 15, Appendices A and E	362-364 381-384 E11, E12
D. Hard drives	7, Appendix E	
4.4 Identify the purpose of CMOS (Complementary Metal-Oxide Semiconductor), what it contains and how to change its basic parameters.	3, 9, Appendix B	
4. Hard drive size and drive type	3, Appendix B	159, 160, B1, B2

Review Questions

Circle True or False.

1. You can identify the location of the pin 1 on a power connector by the red wire. True / False

2. The BIOS must be modified when the hard drive configuration has been changed.
   True / False

3. You should always unplug the hard drive cables while the PC is powered on. True / False

4. Hard drives are not ESD sensitive. True / False

5. Are all IDE hard drive controllers integrated on the systemboard? Explain why or why not.

   _____

   _____

   _____

   _____

   _____

6. Donna wants to install a second hard drive in her PC. She currently has only one IDE controller which has both a hard drive and CD-ROM drive attached to it. Without upgrading the systemboard, describe below how Donna can add a second hard drive to her system and list the hardware she will need to purchase.

   _____

   _____

   _____

   _____

   _____

LAB 7.2 CONFIGURING A DUAL HARD DRIVE SYSTEM

Objective

The objective of this lab exercise is to configure one lab workstation to use two IDE hard drives at the same time. After completing this lab exercise, you will be able to:

- Install, remove, and configure a PC to use one or more IDE hard drives at the same time.
- Understand and describe the difference between the Cable Select and the Master/Slave configurations.

Materials Required

This lab exercise requires a minimum of one lab workstation for every four students. Each workstation should meet the following requirements:

- 486 or better
- 16MB of RAM
- Two IDE hard drives (one should already be installed in the lab workstation)

Two hard drive jumpers (normally already on the hard drives)

One grounding strap for each student

One Cable Select IDE data cable

One grounding mat for each workstation

One standard IDE data cable (Master/Slave)

One Torx bit driver and any other tools necessary to open the lab workstation's case

Lab Setup & Safety Tips

- Each student must be properly grounded using a grounding mat and grounding strap. If students are working in pairs, identify one as Student 1 and the other as Student 2.
- The lab workstation should be previously configured with a standard IDE data cable and one IDE hard drive set to single drive configuration.
- Students must comply with standard ESD procedures.
- Always unplug the power cord before touching any component within the case.

ACTIVITY

Installing a Slave drive using the Master/Slave configuration

Student 1

1. Power off the lab workstation and unplug the power cord (it is not necessary to unplug all other cords).
2. Remove the case from the lab workstation.
3. Locate the hard drive.
4. Unplug the IDE cable and the power connector from the hard drive.
5. Use the Torx bit driver or a screwdriver to dismount the hard drive, if necessary, to view the hard drive jumper configuration.

6. Verify that the installed hard drive is set to Master. (*Note:* Refer to hard drive documentation for a description of jumper settings.)

7. Set the jumper on the second hard drive to the Slave position.

8. Locate an available bay to mount the second hard drive.

9. Mount the second hard drive.

10. Plug in the power connectors to each hard drive.

11. Plug in the IDE data cable to each hard drive.

12. Plug in the power cord and stand clear of the case.

13. With both hard drives plugged in, power on the lab workstation and wait for the BIOS error message.

14. Enter the Setup program and follow the menu instructions for the workstation's BIOS to validate the hard drive changes. Note that the BIOS should now recognize two hard drives.

15. Save the changes and reboot the workstation.

16. Boot into the operating system to verify that it recognizes the additional drive.

Installing a Slave drive using Cable Select

Student 2

1. Power off the lab workstation and unplug the power cord.

2. Unplug the power connectors and the data cables of both IDE hard drives.

3. Unplug the IDE data cable from the systemboard.

4. Connect the Cable Select data cable to the systemboard in the same manner that the standard IDE data cable was connected. (*Note:* The difference between a Cable Select and a standard data cable is that the Cable Select data cable will be marked by a notch or a hole.)

5. Change the jumper settings on both hard drives to the Cable Select position.

6. Plug in the power connectors to each of the IDE hard drives.

7. Remembering that the first hard drive on a Cable Select data cable will be the Master and the second drive will be the Slave, plug in the IDE data cables, and set the original drive as Master.

8. With both hard drives plugged in, power on the lab workstation and wait for the BIOS error message.

9. Enter the Setup program and follow the menu instructions for the workstation's BIOS to validate the hard drive changes. Note that the BIOS should now recognize two hard drives.

10. Save the changes and reboot the workstation.

11. Boot into the operating system to verify that it recognizes the drives correctly.

12. Shut down the workstation and power it off.

13. Unplug the power cable and secure the case.

14. Plug the workstation back in and power it on.

7

Lab Notes

The following is a brief description of the most commonly used jumper settings:

Master—When a drive is set to Master, it will normally be the first hard drive from which the PC will attempt to boot.

Slave—When a drive is set to Slave, it will be the secondary hard drive. This drive is normally referred to as D.

Cable Select—When a drive is configured to use Cable Select, the Master/Slave designation will be determined by the drive's cable position rather than its jumper settings. Using a standard Cable Select data cable, the hard drive connected closest to the systemboard becomes the Master and the drive farthest from the systemboard becomes the Slave.

How is a Cable Select data cable different from other cables?—All Cable Select data cables can easily be recognized as such by a small hole punched somewhere in the data cable. If you cannot locate a small hole punched out somewhere in the data cable, then it is not Cable Select-compliant and you must use the Master/Slave configuration.

How does the Master/Slave configuration work?—When two IDE drives are jumpered to use the Master/Slave configuration, the drives begin sharing one onboard hard drive controller. This means that when a drive is configured as a slave, the electronics for its onboard controller are disabled. The electronics located on the master hard drive then begin to communicate with the IDE controller for both the master and the slave hard drive.

CERTIFICATION OBJECTIVES

Table 7-2   Core A+ Objectives

Objectives	Chapters	Page Numbers
1.2 Identify basic procedures for adding and removing field replaceable modules.	1, 3, 4, 11, 14	
B. Storage device	1, 14	11, 774-779
1.5 Identify proper procedures for installing and configuring IDE/EIDE devices.	6, 7	
A. Master/Slave	6, 7	282, 348-354
B. Devices per channel	6, 7	282, 348-354
1.7 Identify proper procedures for installing and configuring peripheral devices.	14, 15	
C. Storage devices	14	781, 782
2.1 Identify common symptoms and problems associated with each module and how to troubleshoot and isolate the problems.	2, 3, 5, 7, 8, 10, 11, 15, Appendix E	362-364, 381-384, E11, E12
D. Hard drives	7, Appendix E	
4.4 Identify the purpose of CMOS (Complementary Metal-Oxide Semiconductor), what it contains and how to change its basic parameters.	3, 9, Appendix B	
4. Hard drive size and drive type	3, Appendix B	159, 160, B-1, B-2

Review Questions

Circle True or False.

1. When using Cable Select, the location of a hard drive determines whether it will be Master or Slave. True / False

2. You can add as many as three devices to an IDE channel. True / False

3. When two hard drives are present, the Master drive is drive D. True / False

4. How can you easily identify a Cable Select data cable?

   _____

   _____

   _____

   _____

   _____

5. What are the three standard jumper options available with an IDE hard drive?

   _____

   _____

   _____

   _____

   _____

6. How many devices can be attached to an IDE cable?

   _____

   _____

   _____

   _____

   _____

CHAPTER 8

TROUBLESHOOTING FUNDAMENTALS

LABS INCLUDED IN THIS CHAPTER

♦ **LAB 8.1** INPUT/OUTPUT DEVICE TROUBLESHOOTING

♦ **LAB 8.2** BENCHMARKING YOUR PC USING THE NUTS & BOLTS SOFTWARE

♦ **LAB 8.3** HARD DRIVE AND FLOPPY DRIVE TROUBLESHOOTING

♦ **LAB 8.4** TROUBLESHOOTING THE BOOT PROCESS

LAB 8.1 INPUT/OUTPUT DEVICE TROUBLESHOOTING

Objective

The objective of this lab exercise is to familiarize you with some of the common problems that arise during the installation of an input/output device. After completing this lab exercise, you will be able to:

- Install and configure an I/O expansion card.
- Troubleshoot the installation of an I/O expansion card.

Materials Required

This lab exercise requires one complete lab workstation for every two students. Each workstation must have one available ISA slot.

One ISA I/O expansion card for each pair of students (Note that the expansion card should be jumper-configurable rather than jumperless.)

One screwdriver and Torx bit driver for each pair of students

One ESD mat for each lab workstation

One grounding strap for each student

Lab Setup & Safety Tips

- If students are working in pairs, identify one as Student 1 and the other as Student 2.
- Each lab workstation should have the DOS operating system installed and functioning properly.
- Configure the I/O expansion card to use COM3 and COM4.
- Students must comply with standard ESD procedures.
- Always unplug the power cord before touching any component within the case.

ACTIVITY

Installing the expansion card

Student 1

1. Power off the lab workstation and unplug the power cord (it is not necessary to unplug all other cords).

2. Remove the case from the lab workstation.

3. Locate an available ISA slot.

4. Remove the end-of-slot blank.

5. Gently slide the ISA expansion card into the ISA slot; move the card from end to end until it is completely seated. *Warning:* Do not bend the card from side to side.

6. Plug in the power cord.

7. Power on the lab workstation and enter the Setup program.

8. Within the BIOS Setup program, verify that the I/O expansion is recognized by your lab workstation.

9. Exit the BIOS Setup program and reboot the computer.

Creating and Observing an IRQ Conflict

Student 2

1. Power off the lab workstation and remove the I/O expansion card.

2. Unplug the power cord.

3. Gently ease the I/O card out of the ISA slot.

4. Change the COM port selection jumper to COM1.

5. Gently reseat the ISA card; remember to move the card from end to end and not side to side.

6. Plug in the power cord.

7. Power on the lab workstation and observe the results.

> **Lab Notes**
>
> The type of I/O card used in this lab exercise is considered a legacy expansion card. The most commonly used I/O cards are the Plug-and-Play jumperless I/O cards.
>
> Default IRQ settings for PC COM ports are:
>
> **COM1** and **COM3** – IRQ 4
> **COM2** and **COM4** – IRQ 3

CERTIFICATION OBJECTIVES

Table 8-1   Core A+ Objectives

Objectives	Chapters	Page Numbers
1.1 Identify basic terms, concepts, and functions of system modules, including how each module should work during normal operation.	1, 2, 11, 15	
H. BIOS	1	21, 25
I. CMOS	1	8
1.2 Identify basic procedures for adding and removing field replaceable modules.	1, 3, 4, 11, 14	
B. Storage device	1, 14	11, 774-779
1.3 Identify available IRQs, DMAs, and I/O addresses and procedures for configuring them for device installation.	2, 5, 7, 9	
A. Standard IRQ settings	2, 9	83, 90, 463

Review Questions

Circle True or False.

1. COM port settings are always modified using the CMOS Setup program. True / False

2. A COM port won't work properly when it is sharing an IRQ with another COM port. True / False

3. COM4 always uses IRQ 7. True / False

4. COM2 defaults to IRQ 3. True / False

5. COM stands for Communication Office Module. True / False

6. Describe how an IRQ conflict occurs.

_____

_____

_____

_____

_____

LAB 8.2 BENCHMARKING YOUR PC USING THE NUTS & BOLTS SOFTWARE

Objective

The objective of this lab exercise is to benchmark your lab workstation. After completing this lab exercise, you should be able to:

- Benchmark a personal computer's hardware components.
- Use the Nuts & Bolts software package to run hardware diagnostics.

Materials Required

This lab requires one complete lab workstation for every two students. The lab workstation should meet the following requirements:

- 486 or better
- At least 16MB of RAM
- 540MB or larger hard drive
- CD-ROM drive

Each group of students needs one copy of the Nuts & Bolts software included with the textbook.

Lab Setup & Safety Tips

- Each lab workstation should have the Nuts & Bolts software installed and functioning properly.

ACTIVITY

Benchmarking your CPU

1. Power on your lab workstation and allow it to boot into Windows 9x.
2. Click the **Start** button.
3. Click the **Nuts & Bolts** icon.
4. Click the **Discover Pro** icon.
5. Select the **System** tab.
6. Record the following information about your CPU:

   Model _____

   Stepping _____

   L1 cache _____

   L2 cache _____

   Speed in MHZ _____

Benchmarking your hard drive

1. Click the **Start** button.
2. Click the **Nuts & Bolts** icon.
3. Click the **Discover Pro** icon.

4. Select the **Benchmarks** tab.

5. Record the following:

Transfer rates MB/Sec _____

Average seek time Msec _____

Running diagnostics

1. Click the **Start** button.

2. Click the **Nuts & Bolts** icon.

3. Click the **Discover Pro** icon.

4. Select the **Diagnostic** tab.

5. Observe the results.

> **TIP**
>
> ### Lab Notes
>
> **What is Nuts & Bolts?**—The Nuts & Bolts software included with your text-book is a third-party software package designed to help you troubleshoot and benchmark your PC.

CERTIFICATION OBJECTIVES

Table 8-2   Core A+ Objectives

Objectives	Chapters	Page Numbers
1.9 Identify hardware methods of system optimization and when to use them.	3, 4, 6, 7, 9	
A. Memory	4	222
B. Hard drives	6, 7	283-285, 321, 322, 373, 374
C. CPU	3, 9	122, 130, 131, 455, 456
D. Cache memory	3	124
2.2 Identify basic troubleshooting procedures and good practices for eliciting problem symptoms from customers.	8, Appendix A	
A. Troubleshooting/isolation/problem determination procedures.	8	416-420
B. Determine whether hardware or software problem.	8	416-420

Review Questions

Circle True or False.

1. L1 cache and L2 cache are both housed within the CPU. True / False

2. L2 cache is housed inside the processor. True / False

3. CPU speed is measured in megahertz. True / False

4. The Nuts & Bolts software always uses a diagnostic card to test a PC's components. True / False

5. The hard drive seek time is the amount of time it takes your hard drive to locate a particular data cluster. True / False

6. Describe how you would use the Nuts & Bolts software to identify whether a problem is hardware or software related.

_____

_____

_____

_____

_____

8

LAB 8.3 HARD DRIVE AND FLOPPY DRIVE TROUBLESHOOTING

Objective

The objective of this lab exercise is to develop hard drive and floppy drive troubleshooting skills. After completing this lab exercise, you should be able to:

- Troubleshoot all types of PC floppy drive configurations.
- Troubleshoot all types of PC hard drive configurations.
- Describe and implement the troubleshooting process.

Materials Required

This lab requires one complete lab workstation for every four students. The lab workstations should meet the following requirements:

- 486 or better
- At least 16MB of RAM
- 540MB or larger hard drive

One ESD mat for each workstation

One grounding strap for each student

Lab Setup & Safety Tips

- If students are working in pairs, identify one as Student 1 and the other as Student 2.
- Each lab workstation should have Windows 9x installed and functioning properly.

ACTIVITY

Creating problem 1

Student 1

While Student 2 is away from the lab workstation, proceed with the following steps:

1. Power off the lab workstation and unplug the power cord (it is not necessary to unplug all other cords).
2. Remove the case from the lab workstation.
3. Locate the hard drive.
4. Unplug the IDE cable and the power connector from the hard drive.
5. Replace the case.
6. Plug in the power cord.

Troubleshooting and resolving problem 1

Student 2

After Student 1 has reconfigured the lab workstation, power on the workstation, and then answer the following questions and repair the lab workstation.

Are there any error messages? If so, write them down.

_____

_____

_____

What is the problem? Be specific.

_____

_____

_____

_____

_____

List several possible solutions.

_____

_____

_____

_____

_____

Test your theory (solution) and record the results.

_____

_____

_____

_____

_____

How did you discover the problem?

_____

_____

_____

_____

_____

What could you do differently in the future to improve your troubleshooting process?

_____

_____

_____

_____

_____

Creating problem 2

Student 2

While Student 1 is away from the lab workstation, proceed with the following steps:

1. Power off the lab workstation and unplug the power cord (it is not necessary to unplug all other cords).

2. Remove the case from the lab workstation.

3. Locate the floppy drive.

4. Unplug the floppy drive data cable.

5. Using the incorrect connector on the data cable, plug the floppy drive into the data cable.

6. Replace the case.

7. Plug in the power cord.

Troubleshooting and resolving problem 2

Student 1

After Student 2 has reconfigured the lab workstation, power on the workstation, and then answer the following questions and repair the lab workstation.

Are there any error messages? If so, write them down.

_____

_____

_____

_____

_____

What is the problem? Be specific.

_____

_____

_____

_____

_____

List several possible solutions.

_____

_____

_____

_____

_____

Test your theory (solution) and record the results.

_____

_____

_____

_____

_____

How did you discover the problem?

_____

_____

_____

_____

_____

What could you do differently in the future to improve your troubleshooting process?

_____

_____

_____

_____

_____

Lab Notes

The six steps of the troubleshooting process are:

1. Let the customer explain the problem.
2. Search for answers.
3. Develop a hypothesis.
4. Test your theory.
5. Resolve the problem and explain your changes to the customer.
6. Complete proper documentation.

What is troubleshooting documentation?—Troubleshooting documentation includes any documentation required by your employer and/or your own collection of notes and files.

8

A+ CERTIFICATION OBJECTIVES

Table 8-3 Core A+ Objectives

Objectives	Chapters	Page Numbers
2.1 Identify common symptoms and problems associated with each module and how to troubleshoot and isolate the problems.	2, 3, 5, 7, 8, 10, 11, 15, Appendices A and E	
D. Hard drives	7, Appendix E	362-364, 381-384, E11, E12
N. POST audible/visual error codes	8, 11	409, 410, 566-568
2.2 Identify basic troubleshooting procedures and good practices for eliciting problem symptoms from customers.	8, Appendix A	
A. Troubleshooting/isolation/problem determination procedures.	8	416-420
B. Determine whether hardware or software problem.	8	416-420
E. Symptoms/Error Codes	8, Appendix A	416-420, A1, A2
F. Situation when the problem occurred	8	416-421

Review Questions

Circle **True** or **False**.

1. You should always verify that your sound card is functioning properly before troubleshooting a hard drive problem. **True / False**

2. While you are troubleshooting a problem, it is best to make only one change at a time. **True / False**

3. List three of the six troubleshooting steps below.

_____

_____

_____

_____

_____

4. Describe how a floppy drive will behave if it is not plugged in correctly.

_____

_____

_____

_____

_____

LAB 8.4 TROUBLESHOOTING THE BOOT PROCESS

Objective

The objective of this lab exercise is to further develop your troubleshooting skills and master the PC boot process. After completing this lab exercise, you should be able to:

- Successfully troubleshoot all types of PC configurations.
- Describe and implement the troubleshooting process, and explain how it pertains to the PC boot process.

Materials Required

This lab requires one complete lab workstation for every four students. The lab workstations should meet the following requirements:

- 486 or better
- At least 16MB of RAM
- 540MB or larger hard drive
- CD-ROM drive

One ESD mat for each lab workstation

One grounding strap for each student

Lab Setup & Safety Tips

- If students are working in pairs, identify one as Student 1 and the other as Student 2.
- Each lab workstation should have Windows 9x installed and functioning properly.

ACTIVITY

Creating problem 1

Student 1

While Student 2 is away from the lab workstation, proceed with the following steps:

1. Power off the lab workstation and unplug the power cord (it is not necessary to unplug all other cords).
2. Remove the case from the lab workstation.
3. Unplug the P8 and P9 connectors from the systemboard.
4. Replace the case.
5. Plug in the power cord.

Troubleshooting and resolving problem 1

Student 2

After Student 1 has reconfigured the lab workstation, power on the workstation, and then answer the following questions and repair the lab workstation.

Are there any error messages? If so, write them down.

_____

_____

_____

_____

_____

What is the problem? Be specific.

_____

_____

_____

_____

_____

List several possible solutions.

_____

_____

_____

_____

_____

Test your theory (solution) and record the results.

_____

_____

_____

_____

_____

How did you discover the problem?

_____

_____

_____

_____

_____

What could you do differently in the future to improve your troubleshooting process?

_____

_____

_____

_____

_____

Creating problem 2

Student 2

While Student 1 is away from the lab workstation, proceed with the following steps:

1. Power off the lab workstation and unplug the power cord (it is not necessary to unplug all other cords).

2. Remove the case from the lab workstation.

3. Locate the hard drive.

4. Move the jumper of the hard drive to the Slave position.

5. Replace the case.

6. Plug in the power cord.

Troubleshooting and resolving problem 2

Student 1

After Student 2 has reconfigured the lab workstation, power on the workstation, and then answer the following questions and repair the lab workstation.

Are there any error messages? If so, write them down.

_____

_____

_____

_____

_____

What is the problem? Be specific.

_____

_____

_____

_____

List several possible solutions.

_____

_____

_____

_____

Test your theory (solution) and record the results.

_____

_____

_____

_____

8

How did you discover the problem?

_____

_____

_____

_____

What could you do differently in the future to improve your troubleshooting process?

_____

_____

_____

_____

Lab Notes

Which way should the P8 and P9 connectors be attached?—When connecting the P8 and P9 power connectors, remember that the ground, or the black wires, should always face each other.

How do I improve my troubleshooting skills?—Troubleshooting is a skill that takes time and experience to develop. Exercises like this one will help you improve your troubleshooting skills by providing you that experience without the pressure of a customer's expectations. When you see a new error message, rather than avoiding the problem, become a relentless investigator and search for the answer. Your troubleshooting skills and experience will grow exponentially from the process of your investigations.

What does POST stand for?—POST is an acronym for Power On Self Test. This is the time during the boot process when the BIOS tests all essential hardware.

 ## CERTIFICATION OBJECTIVES

Table 8-4   Core A+ Objectives

Objectives	Chapters	Page Numbers
2.1 Identify common symptoms and problems associated with each module and how to troubleshoot and isolate the problems.	2, 3, 5, 7, 8, 10, 11, 15, Appendices A and E	
D. Hard drives	7, Appendix E	362-364, 381-384, E11, E12
N. POST audible/visual error codes	8, 11	409, 410, 566-568
2.2 Identify basic troubleshooting procedures and good practices for eliciting problem symptoms from customers.	8, Appendix A	
A. Troubleshooting/isolation/problem determination procedures.	8	416-420
B. Determine whether hardware or software problem.	8	416-420
E. Symptoms/Error Codes	8, Appendix A	416-420, A1, A2
F. Situation when the problem occurred	8	416-421

Review Questions

Circle True or False.

1. Always ask the customer to leave when you are going to troubleshoot a PC. True / False

2. Asking the customer questions almost always helps you resolve their problem more quickly. True / False

3. If a problem is detected during POST, the BIOS will normally return an error message. True / False

4. If a problem is detected during POST, it is most likely software related. True / False

5. POST stands for _____.

6. Describe the symptoms of an unplugged hard drive.

   _____

   _____

   _____

   _____

   _____

8

INPUT/OUTPUT DEVICES

LABS INCLUDED IN THIS CHAPTER

♦ LAB 9.1 SERIAL PORT CONFLICT RESOLUTION

♦ LAB 9.2 PARALLEL PORT CONFLICT RESOLUTION

♦ LAB 9.3 SCSI ADAPTER INSTALLATION

♦ LAB 9.4 SCSI CHAIN CONFLICT RESOLUTION

LAB 9.1 SERIAL PORT CONFLICT RESOLUTION

Objective

Serial port conflicts commonly occur when an internal modem is installed in a PC. You can approach troubleshooting these conflicts in several ways, depending on the environment. This lab exercise shows you how to properly troubleshoot a serial port conflict in the Windows 9x environment. After completing this lab exercise, you will be able to:

- Define a serial port conflict.
- Describe the symptoms of a serial port conflict.
- Use the Device Manager to discover which device is conflicting with the serial port.
- Resolve serial port conflicts.

Materials Required

This lab exercise requires one complete lab workstation for every four students. The lab workstation should meet the following requirements:

- 486 or better
- 16MB of RAM
- Windows 9x
- One jumpered internal modem, including documentation for the internal modem's jumper settings (a phone line is not necessary)
- At least one COM port

One ESD mat for each lab workstation

Grounding straps for each student

Lab Setup & Safety Tips

- Each lab workstation should have Windows 9x installed and functioning properly.
- Each lab workstation should have an internal modem installed and functioning properly.
- Each lab workstation's modem should be configured to use COM2.
- Each lab workstation's COM port should be configured to use COM1.
- Students must comply with standard ESD procedures.

ACTIVITY

Creating and observing the conflict

1. Power off the lab workstation.

2. Unplug the power cord.

3. Remove the case from the lab workstation.

4. Locate the modem.

5. Using the documentation provided, change the modem jumper settings from COM2 to COM1.

6. Replace the case and plug in the power cord.

7. Power on your lab workstation and allow it to boot into Windows 9x. Note that depending on the type of system, you might receive an error message during the POST. Observe any error messages and continue booting the system by following the instructions on the screen.

8. Click the **Start** button, point to **Settings**, then click **Control Panel**.

9. Double-click the **System** icon.

10. Click the **Device Manager** tab.

11. Look for yellow exclamation points located on top of COM1 and the modem icon. If you see the yellow exclamation marks, you have successfully created a resource conflict between the two devices.

Resolving the conflict

You can resolve this conflict in several ways. The needs of the user will determine the best method. For example, you already know that you can easily resolve this conflict simply by changing the modem jumper settings back to the original settings. Another solution would be to disable or reassign the COM port's resources.

Reassigning or disabling the COM port's resources

1. Reboot your lab workstation.

2. Enter the BIOS Setup program.

3. Locate the serial configuration section.

4. Change your serial port configuration from COM2 to Disabled.

5. Save the changes and reboot the lab workstation.

Note: Not all serial ports are configurable through the BIOS. If the COM port configuration is not available through the BIOS Setup program of your lab workstation, ask your instructor for the I/O card configuration.

Table 9-1 Default port assignments on many computers

Port	IRQ	Type	I/O Address
COM1	IRQ 4	Serial	03F8
COM2	IRQ 3	Serial	02F8
COM3	IRQ 4	Serial	03E8
COM4	IRQ 3	Serial	02E8
LPT1:	IRQ 7	Parallel	0378
LPT2:	IRQ 5	Parallel	0278

Lab Notes

Note that in some of the more severe cases, a PC completely freezes when a serial port conflict occurs.

Viewing device resources—You can use the Device Manager to view resource settings by double-clicking the device icon.

Yellow exclamation marks in the Device Manager?—When the Device Manager displays a yellow exclamation mark over a device, it means that the device is conflicting with another device.

A red "X" in the Device Manager?—When the Device Manger displays a red "X" over a device, this means that the device has been disabled in the current hardware profile.

A^+ **CERTIFICATION OBJECTIVES**

Table 9-2   Core A+ Objectives

Objectives	Chapters	Page Numbers
1.1 Identify basic terms, concepts, and functions of system modules, including how each module should work during normal operation.	1, 2, 11, 15	
E. Modem	1, 15	18, 803, 804
2.1 Identify common symptoms and problems associated with each module and how to troubleshoot and isolate the problems.	2, 3, 5, 7, 8, 10, 11, 15, Appendices A and E	
H. Modems	15	838-841
N. POST audible/visual error codes	8, Appendix A	424, A1, A2
4.4 Identify the purpose of CMOS (Complementary Metal-Oxide Semiconductor), what it contains and how to change its basic parameters.	3, 9, Appendix B	
2. COM/serial port	3	159, 169
a. memory address	9	462, 463
b. interrupt request	9	462, 463
c. disable	9	462, 463

Table 9-3   DOS/Windows A+ Objectives

Objectives	Chapters	Page Numbers
4.3 Recognize common problems and determine how to resolve them.	1, 4, 5, 8, 12, 16, Appendix E	
A. Common problems		
4. System lock up	12, Appendix E	613, E28
B. DOS and Windows- based utilities		
2. Device manager	12	647, 648

Review Questions

Circle True or False.

1. The Device Manager can be found by opening the Control Panel and then clicking the Network icon. True / False

2. A red "X" in the Device Manager means that the device is disabled. True / False

3. All serial ports can be configured using the BIOS Setup program. True / False

4. Serial ports can conflict only with modems. True / False

5. To what IRQ does COM4 default?

_____

6. Describe how to view the IRQ of a device using the Device Manager.

_____

_____

_____

_____

7. List two ways to resolve a serial conflict.

8. You are the desktop PC support technician for the Good Job Corporation. Janet, one of your customers, suspects that she has a resource conflict between her newly installed modem and one of the serial ports on her laptop. Describe how you would use the Device Manager to confirm or eliminate her suspicions.

9. Steve, one of your customers, just installed an I/O card into his PC because he needs more than two COM ports. He now receives an error message every time he starts his system. Steve asks you to troubleshoot. Describe the steps you take to resolve Steve's conflict.

9

Lab 9.2 Parallel Port Conflict Resolution

Objective

Parallel port conflicts commonly occur when a sound card is installed into a PC. In this lab exercise, you examine the process of locating and resolving a parallel port conflict. After completing this lab exercise, you will be able to:

- Define a parallel port conflict.
- Describe the symptoms of a parallel port conflict.
- Use the Device Manager to discover which device is causing the parallel port conflict.
- Resolve parallel port conflicts.

Materials Required

This lab exercise requires one complete lab workstation for every four students. The lab workstations should meet the following requirements:

- 486 or better
- 16MB of RAM
- Windows 9x
- One 8- or 16-bit sound card
- At least one LPT port

One ESD mat
Grounding straps for each student
Documentation containing your sound card's jumper settings

Lab Setup & Safety Tips

- Each lab workstation should have Windows 9x installed and functioning properly.
- Each lab workstation should have a sound card installed and functioning properly.
- Each lab workstation's sound card should be configured to use IRQ 5.
- LPT1 should be configured to use default settings.
- Students must comply with standard ESD procedures.

Activity

Creating and Observing the conflict

1. Power off the lab workstation.

2. Unplug the power cord.

3. Remove the case from the lab workstation.

4. Locate the sound card.

5. Using the documentation provided, change the sound card jumper settings from IRQ 5 to IRQ 7.

6. Replace the case and plug in the power cord.

7. Power on your lab workstation and allow it to boot to Windows 9x. Note that depending on the type of system, you might receive an error message during the POST. Observe any error messages and continue to boot the system by following the instructions on the screen.

8. Click the **Start** button, point to **Settings**, and then click **Control Panel**.

9. Double-click the **System** icon.

10. Click the **Device Manager** tab.

11. Look for yellow exclamation points located on top of LPT1 and the sound card icon. If you see the yellow exclamation points, you have successfully created a resource conflict between the two devices.

Resolving the Conflict

You can resolve a parallel port conflict in several ways. Like serial conflicts, you also can resolve a parallel conflict simply by disabling the parallel port. Under most circumstances, however, you cannot disable the parallel port because the user needs it for the printer. This leaves you with two options. One is to reassign the resources of the conflicting device, and the other is to reassign the resources of the parallel port.

Reassigning or disabling the parallel port's resources

1. Reboot your lab workstation.

2. Enter the BIOS Setup program.

3. Locate the parallel configuration section.

4. Change your parallel port resources settings to IRQ 5, and be sure to use a different I/O address.

5. Save the changes and reboot the lab workstation.

Verifying the resource conflict has been resolved

1. Power on your lab workstation and allow it to boot into Windows 9x.

2. Click the **Start** button, point to **Settings**, and then click **Control Panel**.

3. Double-click the **System** icon.

4. Click the **Device Manager** tab.

5. Double-click **Ports**.

6. Double-click **LPT1**.

7. Click the **Resources** tab.

Note that the IRQ and I/O settings now read what you previously chose in the BIOS Setup program.

8. Click the **Cancel** button.

9. Double-click **Sound, video,** and **game controllers**.

10. Double-click the **sound card** icon.

11. Click the **Resources** tab.

12. Observe the IRQ and I/O settings of the sound card.

Note: Not all parallel ports can be configured through the BIOS. If the parallel port configuration is not available through the BIOS Setup program of your lab workstation, ask your instructor for the proper configuration.

Lab Notes

COM port assignment vs. LPT assignment—Unlike COM ports, parallel ports do not allow you to simply change the LPT number from LPT1 to LPT2 and maintain the same system resources. You can assign a COM port number (1, 2, 3, 4) to any I/O address and IRQ that are reserved for COM use. However, the BIOS assigns a parallel port its LPT number (1, 2, 3) in the order of highest I/O address first.

Do parallel ports work only on printers?—Parallel communication was originally intended for use with printers only. However, because parallel port communication is faster than serial communication, it is commonly used for fast data transfers over short distances. To accomplish this sort of data transfer, a *bi-directional* parallel port is used.

CERTIFICATION OBJECTIVES

Table 9-4   Core A+ Objectives

Objectives	Chapters	Page Numbers
1.3 Identify available IRQs, DMAs, and I/O addresses and procedures for configuring them for device installation.	2, 5, 7, 9	
A. Standard IRQ settings	2, 9	83, 90, 463
1.4 Identify common peripheral ports, associated cabling, and their connectors.	1, 9, 15, 16	
A. Cable types	1	19
B. Cable orientation	9	462
C. Serial versus parallel	1, 9	19, 463, 469-471
D. Pin connections		
1. DB-9	9	462
2. DB-25	9	462
2.1 Identify common symptoms and problems associated with each module and how to troubleshoot and isolate the problems.	2, 3, 5, 7, 8, 10, 11, 15, Appendices A and E	
F. Sound Card/Audio	10, Appendix E	543, E26
J. BIOS	2, 3	89, 135-138
K. CMOS	3	159, 160, 420, 421, 424, 428
M. Slot covers	14	781-784
N. POST audible/visual error codes	8, Appendix A	424, A1, A2
4.4 Identify the purpose of CMOS (Complementary Metal-Oxide Semiconductor), what it contains and how to change its basic parameters.	3, 9, Appendix B	
1. **Printer parallel port**	9	469-471
a. Uni., bi-directional	9	469-471
b. disable/enable	9	469-471
c. ECP	9	469-471
d. EPP	9	469-471

Review Questions

Circle True or False.

1. Parallel ports are assigned their LPT number by the BIOS. True / False

2. Parallel ports do not need an IRQ. True / False

3. You can have only one parallel port per computer. True / False

4. Serial ports commonly conflict with parallel ports. True / False

5. Briefly describe how parallel ports are assigned LPT numbers.

   _____

   _____

   _____

   _____

   _____

6. List two ways a parallel port conflict can be resolved.

   _____

   _____

   _____

   _____

   _____

7. You are working on a PC that has the parallel port built into the systemboard. You are about to install a new sound card that will use IRQ 7. Describe the steps you need to take to avoid an IRQ conflict with the sound card.

   _____

   _____

   _____

   _____

   _____

9

Lab 9.3 SCSI Adapter Installation

Objective

The objective of this lab exercise is to properly install and configure a SCSI host adapter. After completing this lab exercise, you will be able to:

- Properly install a SCSI host adapter.

- Describe several ways to use SCSI host adapters.

- Use the Device Manager to view a SCSI host adapter's resources.

- Describe the difference between the SCSI BIOS Setup program and the system CMOS Setup program.

Materials Required

This lab exercise requires one complete lab workstation for every four students. The lab workstations should meet the following requirements:

- 486 or better

- 16MB of RAM

- Windows 9x

One SCSI host adapter for each lab workstation

One ESD mat

Grounding straps for each student

Several disks containing the necessary Windows 9x drivers for each SCSI card

Documentation containing your SCSI card's jumper settings

Lab Setup & Safety Tips

- The instructor will provide the students with the proper resource settings for their lab workstations.

- Each lab workstation should have Windows 9x installed and functioning properly.

- Students must comply with standard ESD procedures.

- Always unplug the power cord before touching any component within the case.

ACTIVITY

Installing the SCSI Host Adapter

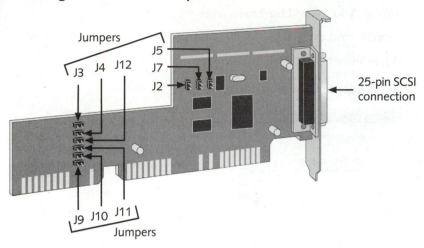

Figure 9-1 SCSI host adapter for one single-ended device

1. Power off the lab workstation.

2. Unplug the power cord.

3. Remove the case from the lab workstation.

4. Locate an available expansion slot for your SCSI host adapter.

5. Using the documentation provided, verify that your SCSI card is configured to your instructor's resource specifications.

6. Insert the SCSI card, illustrated in Figure 9-1, into an appropriate slot, and then secure the card using a screw.

7. Replace the case and plug in the power cord.

8. Power on your lab workstation and allow it to boot to Windows 9x.

9. While Windows 9x is booting, note whether it automatically detects the new SCSI card.

If Windows 9x detects the SCSI card and prompts you for the drivers,

1. Insert the driver disk.

2. Click the **Drivers provided by the hardware manufacturer** option button.

3. Click the **OK** button.

4. Click the **Browse** button to locate the drivers on the disk.

5. Click **OK**.

6. Select the driver for the SCSI card that you installed.

7. Click **OK**.

8. If you are prompted for the Windows 9x cab files, click the **Browse** button to locate them.

If Windows 9x does not detect the SCSI card

1. Click the **Start** button, point to **Settings**, and then click **Control Panel**.

2. Double-click the **Add New Hardware** icon.

3. Click the **Next** button three times to allow Windows 9x to detect the SCSI card.

4. Install the driver from the disk when prompted.

Verifying the SCSI host adapter driver installation

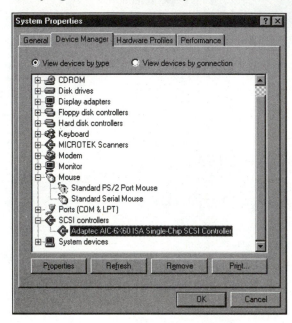

Figure 9-2   Device Manager displays the newly installed host adapter

1. Click the **Start** button, point to **Settings**, and then click **Control Panel**.

2. Double-click the **System** icon.

3. Click the **Device Manager** tab illustrated in Figure 9-2.

4. Double-click the **SCSI Controllers** icon.

5. Verify that the SCSI host adapter driver is properly installed without any errors (there shouldn't be any yellow exclamation points).

Viewing the SCSI Setup program

1. Reboot your lab workstation. After the standard system POST is complete, you should see a SCSI BIOS screen.

2. Follow the directions on the SCSI BIOS screen and enter the SCSI CMOS Setup program.

3. Follow the directions for the SCSI BIOS and observe the options.

Lab Notes

Different types of SCSI host adapters—There are several types of SCSI host adapters, ranging from single proprietary host adapters to large-scale host adapters that support many SCSI devices.

Configuring a PC to use both IDE and SCSI hard drives—Configuring a PC to use both an IDE and a SCSI hard drive at the same time is relatively simple. First, configure the IDE drive as Master. Second, configure the SCSI drive to use an available SCSI ID. Remember that on a PC with both IDE and SCSI, the IDE drive must be drive C, because the system BIOS loads before the SCSI BIOS.

What is the difference between SCSI and IDE?—One of the most important differences between SCSI and IDE is that the SCSI is substantially faster than the IDE.

 ## CERTIFICATION OBJECTIVES

9

Table 9-5   Core A+ Objectives

Objectives	Chapters	Page Numbers
1.6 Identify proper procedures for installing and configuring SCSI devices.		
D. Internal versus external	18	994, 995
E. Switch and jumper settings	7	365, 366, 782-784

Table 9-6   DOS/Windows A+ Objectives

Objectives	Chapters	Page Numbers
3.1 Identify the procedures for installing DOS, Windows 3.x, and Windows 95, and for bringing the software to a basic operational level.	6, 7, 12	
D. Loading drivers	12	611, 612
3.4 Identify procedures for loading/adding device drivers and the necessary software for certain devices.	4, 9, 10	
B. Windows 95 Plug and Play	9, 10	459-461, 526

Review Questions

Circle True or False.

1. SCSI is faster than IDE. True / False

2. To install a SCSI host adapter on a PC, there must be one available IRQ. True / False

3. All SCSI hard drives have a built-in BIOS. True / False

4. You can modify the SCSI BIOS through the system BIOS. True / False

5. When a PC is configured to use both SCSI and IDE, which drive must be drive C, and why?

_____

_____

_____

_____

6. You are working as a desktop PC support technician at the Black Moon Company. Carol, one of your customers, asks you to install a SCSI host adapter into her computer. Describe the steps necessary to complete the job for Carol.

_____

_____

_____

_____

_____

LAB 9.4 SCSI CHAIN CONFLICT RESOLUTION

Objective

The objective of this lab exercise is to troubleshoot and resolve a SCSI chain conflict. After completing this lab exercise, you will be able to:

- Describe how a SCSI chain conflict occurs.

- Install and configure a SCSI hard drive.

- Properly identify a SCSI chain conflict.

- Resolve a SCSI chain conflict.

Materials Required

This lab exercise requires one complete lab workstation for every four students. The lab workstations should meet the following requirements:

- 486 or better

- 16MB of RAM

- Windows 9x

- One SCSI host adapter installed

Two SCSI hard drives for each lab workstation

One ESD mat

Grounding straps for each student

Documentation for each SCSI hard drive jumper configuration

Lab Setup & Safety Tips

- Each lab workstation should have Windows 9x installed and functioning properly.

- Students must comply with standard ESD procedures.

- Always unplug the power cord before touching any component within the case.

- One SCSI hard drive should be properly installed and configured prior to starting the lab exercise.

- The previously installed IDE hard drive should be configured as drive C and contain the operating system.

ACTIVITY

Creating the SCSI chain conflict

For the purpose of this lab exercise, the installed SCSI hard drive will be referred to as SCSI drive. The second SCSI hard drive, used to create the conflict, will be referred to as SCSI drive 2.

1. Power off the lab workstation.

2. Unplug the power cord.

3. Remove the case from the lab workstation.

4. Using the jumper documentation provided, set both SCSI hard drives to the same SCSI ID.

5. Mount SCSI drive 2.

6. Plug in the power and data cables to SCSI drive 2.

7. Stand clear of the case and plug in the power cord.

8. Power on your lab workstation and allow it to boot into Windows 9x.

9. Observe the error messages during the boot process.

Resolving the SCSI chain conflict

1. Power off the lab workstation.

2. Unplug the power cord.

3. Locate SCSI drive 2.

4. Dismount SCSI drive 2.

5. Unplug the power and data cables.

6. Using the jumper documentation provided, set SCSI drive 2 to an available SCSI ID.

7. Mount SCSI drive 2.

8. Plug in the power and data cables to SCSI drive 2.

9. Replace the case and plug in the power cord.

10. Power on the lab workstation and enter the SCSI BIOS Setup program.

11. Verify that the SCSI BIOS correctly recognizes both SCSI drives.

12. Exit the Setup program and reboot the lab workstation.

13. Allow your lab workstation to boot into Windows 9x.

14. Double-click the **My Computer** icon.

15. Verify that Windows 9x recognizes both SCSI hard drives.

Lab Notes

What is SCAM?—SCAM stands for SCSI configuration automatically. It is a method by which SCSI devices and the host adapter are Plug-and-Play-compliant, so the user does not need to manually set the ID on the device.

What is termination all about?—SCSI devices require some sort of termination to prevent signal bounce. You can use one of several types of terminators. Each terminator varies in quality and compatibility. Some SCSI devices are self-terminating. Consult your SCSI host adapter documentation for proper termination specifications.

CERTIFICATION OBJECTIVES

Table 9-7   Core A+ Objectives

Objectives	Chapters	Page Numbers
1.6 Identify proper procedures for installing and configuring SCSI devices.	6, 7, 9, 18	
A. Address/Termination conflicts	6	287-290
B. Cabling	6, 7	288, 289, 292, 348
C. Types (example: regular, wide, ultra-wide)	6, 9	287-289, 481-485
D. Internal versus external	18	994, 995
E. Switch and jumper settings	7	365, 366, 782-784

Table 9-8   DOS/Windows A+ Objectives

Objectives	Chapters	Page Numbers
3.1 Identify the procedures for installing DOS, Windows 3.x, and Windows 95, and for bringing the software to a basic operational level.	6, 7, 12	
D. Loading drivers	12	611, 612
3.4 Identify procedures for loading/adding device drivers and the necessary software for certain devices.		
B. Windows 95 Plug and Play	9, 10	459-461, 526

Review Questions

Circle True or False.

1. A SCSI chain conflict occurs when a SCSI device is not plugged into the SCSI cable.
   True / False

2. A SCSI chain conflict occurs when two or more SCSI drives are set to Master. True / False

3. All SCSI devices require some sort of termination. True / False

4. SCAM stands for SCSI Configuration Automatically. True / False

5. How is SCAM helpful?

   _____

   _____

   _____

   _____

   _____

6. You are working as a desktop PC support technician at the Black Moon Company. Bob, one of your customers, wants you to give him written directions for installing and configuring a SCSI hard drive. Write the instructions you would give to Bob.

   _____

   _____

   _____

   _____

   _____

9

MULTIMEDIA TECHNOLOGY

LABS INCLUDED IN THIS CHAPTER

LAB 10.1 MULTIMEDIA VIDEO

Objective

The objective of this lab exercise is to install and configure a video adapter card. After completing this lab exercise, you will be able to:

- Install a video adapter card.
- Install drivers for a video adapter card.
- Configure a video adapter card.

Materials Required

This lab exercise requires one complete lab workstation for every four students. The lab workstation should meet the following requirements:

- 486 or better
- 16MB of RAM
- Windows 9x

One video adapter for each lab workstation

Necessary drivers for each video adapter card

Tools necessary to remove the case and install a video adapter card

Lab Setup & Safety Tips

- Each lab workstation should have Windows 9x installed and functioning properly.
- Students must comply with standard ESD procedures.
- Always unplug the power cord before touching any component in the case.

ACTIVITY

Installing the video adapter card

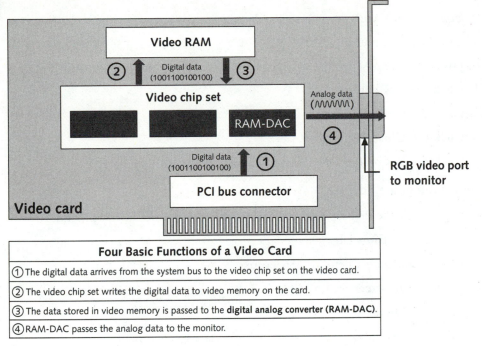

Figure 10-1   Four basic functions of a video card

1. Power off the lab workstation and unplug the power cord.

2. Remove the case from the lab workstation.

3. Locate an available PCI slot. *Note*: Video adapters normally use the ACI bus because it is faster than the ISA bus.

4. Remove the end–of–slot blank.

5. Gently slide the PCI expansion card into the PCI slot, moving the card from end to end until it is completely seated. *Warning*: Do not bend the card from side to side.

6. Plug in the power cord.

7. Stand clear of the case and power on the lab workstation. If you can view the POST screen, then the adapter has been properly installed.

8. Power off the lab workstation and unplug the power cord.

9. Replace the case.

10. Plug in the power cord.

11. Power on the lab workstation and allow it to boot into Windows 9x.

Installing the video driver

1. Right–click the desktop, and select **Properties** from the shortcut menu.

2. Click the **Settings** tab.

3. Click the **Advanced** button.

4. Click the **Change** button next to the Adapter Type heading.

5. In the Update Device Driver Wizard, click **Next**.

10

6. Click to select the **Display a list of all the drivers in a specific location** option, and then click **Next**.

7. Click the **Have Disk** button.

8. Insert the disk with the video drivers.

9. Click the **OK** button.

10. From the menu, select the video adapter driver that you want to use.

11. Click the **OK** button.

12. Click the **Close** button.

13. Click the **Close** button.

14. Click the **Yes** button when prompted to restart your computer.

Configuring the video adapter

1. Right-click the desktop, and select **Properties** from the shortcut menu.

2. Click the **Settings** tab.

3. Change the color palette to **256 colors**.

4. Change your screen area to **1024 X 768**.

5. Click the **OK** button.

6. Click the **Yes** button when prompted to restart your computer.

Lab Notes

What is display resolution and dot pitch?—Display resolution is the measure of pixels on the screen that are addressable by software. Dot pitch is the distance between each adjacent pixel. The smaller the dot pitch, the closer together each pixel, and the more clear your image will appear.

Table 10-1   Features of a monitor

Monitor Characteristic	Description
Screen size	Screens are usually described as 14-inch, 16-inch, 17-inch, 21-inch, or larger. This screen size usually refers to the diagonal length of the lighted area, although the measurement is not particularly accurate. The actual diagonal length is usually shorter than the advertised measurement.
Refresh rate	Refresh rate, or vertical scan rate, is the time it takes for an electronic beam to fill a video screen with lines from top to bottom. A Super VGA monitor must have a minimum refresh rate of 70 Hz, or 70 times per second.
Interlaced	Rather than drawing the entire screen on every pass, interlaced monitors only refresh half the screen on every pass: the first pass draws the odd lines and the second pass draws the even lines. Compared to noninterlaced monitors, interlaced monitors do not provide the same quality for the same refresh rate, although, because of interlacing, the overall effect is less noticeable.

Table 10-1   Features of a monitor (continued)

Monitor Characteristic	Description
Dot pitch	Dot pitch is the distance between adjacent dots on the screen. The smaller the dot pitch, the higher the quality of the image. A high-quality monitor should have a dot pitch of no more than .28 mm.
Display Resolution	A measure of how many spots, or pixels, on the screen are addressable by software. The video controller card as well as the monitor must be capable of supporting the chosen resolution. A common resolution is 800 by 600. Resolutions are set from the Control Panel in Windows.
Multiscan	Monitors that offer a variety of refresh rates are called multiscan monitors. Multiscan monitors can support different video cards, whereas fixed frequency monitors only support a single refresh rate.
Green monitor	A green monitor supports the EPA Energy Star program. When a screen saver is on, the monitor should use no more than 30 watts of electricity.

Lab Notes

What is VRAM?—Video RAM, or VRAM, is RAM on a video card that allows simultaneous access from both the input and output processes.

What is WRAM?—WRAM is dual-ported Video RAM that is faster and less expensive than VRAM. It has its own internal bus on the chip with a data path that is 256 bits wide.

10

CERTIFICATION OBJECTIVES

Table 10-2   Core A+ Objectives

Objectives	Chapters	Page Numbers
1.7 Identify proper procedures for installing and configuring peripheral devices.	14, 15	
A. Monitor/Video Card	14	765, 766
2.1 Identify common symptoms and problems associated with each module and how to troubleshoot and isolate the problems.	2, 3, 5, 7, 8, 10, 11, 15, Appendices A and E	
F. Monitor/Video	8, Appendix E	420, 421, 430-434, E15, E17
4.2 Identify the categories of RAM (Random Access Memory) terminology, their locations, and physical characteristics.	3, 4, 9	
A. **Terminology:**		
4. VRAM (Video RAM)	9	500
5. WRAM (Windows Accelerator Card RAM)	9	500, 501

Table 10-3   DOS/Windows A+ Objectives

Objectives	Chapters	Page Numbers
3.1 Identify the procedures for installing DOS, Windows 3.x, and Windows 95, and for bringing the software to a basic operational level.	6, 7, 12	
D. Loading drivers	12	611, 612
3.4 Identify procedures for loading/adding device drivers and the necessary software for certain devices.	4, 9, 10	
A. Windows 3.x procedures	4	198, 199
B. Windows 95 Plug and Play	9, 10	459-461, 526

Review Questions

Circle True or False.

1. Video adapters normally use the PCI bus because it is faster than the ISA bus. True / False

2. All video cards have the same display capabilities. True / False

3. VRAM stands for Virtual RAM, which is commonly found on a video card. True / False

4. If Windows 9x doesn't have the video driver for your video adapter, you can install the correct video driver by using the Have Disk button and loading the driver from another location. True / False

5. Describe the relationship between VRAM and your display resolution and color quality.

   _____

   _____

   _____

   _____

   _____

6. Jimmy has just installed a new video adapter, but now his monitor is blank. Is Jimmy's problem hardware or software related? List the first three troubleshooting steps you would take if you were in Jimmy's position.

   _____

   _____

   _____

   _____

   _____

LAB 10.2 INSTALLING AND CONFIGURING AN IDE CD-ROM DRIVE

Objective

The objective of this lab exercise is to install and configure a CD-ROM drive. After completing this lab exercise, you will be able to:

- Install an IDE CD-ROM drive.
- Describe how to load a device driver for an IDE CD-ROM drive.

Materials Required

This lab exercise requires one complete lab workstation for every four students. The lab workstation should meet the following requirements:

- 486 or better
- 16MB of RAM
- Windows 9x
- 850MB hard drive

One CD-ROM drive for each lab workstation

Tools necessary to remove the case and install a CD-ROM drive

Lab Setup & Safety Tips

- Each lab workstation should have Windows 9x installed and functioning properly.
- The installation files for Windows 9x should be copied to the hard drive of each lab workstation.
- Students must comply with standard ESD procedures.
- Always unplug the power cord before touching any component in the case.

ACTIVITY

Installing an IDE CD-ROM Drive

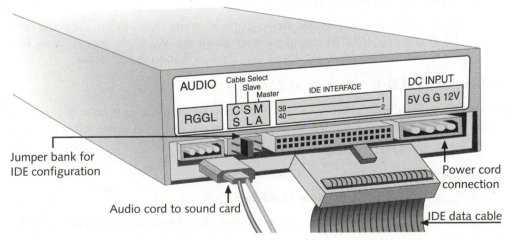

Figure 10-2   Rear view of an IDE CD-ROM drive

10

1. Power off the lab workstation and unplug the power cord.

2. Remove the case from the lab workstation.

3. Locate an available 5¼-inch drive bay.

4. Remove from the front of the case any blank that may be present.

5. Verify that the hard drive is set to Master.

6. Change the CD-ROM jumper to Slave.

7. Slide the CD-ROM drive into the drive bay and use the screw to mount it to the inside of the case.

8. Connect the IDE data cable and be sure that the red stripe is aligned with pin one. (*Note*: Sometimes the stripe is blue.)

9. Plug in the four-pronged power cord.

10. If there is a sound card present, connect the audio cable to the back of the CD-ROM drive.

Verify that the workstation boots properly

1. Stand back from the case and plug in the power cord.

2. Turn on the workstation and verify that the system boots properly. If the workstation doesn't boot properly, the jumpers might be set incorrectly.

3. Power off the workstation.

4. Remove the power cord.

5. Replace the case.

6. Plug in the power cord.

Testing an IDE CD-ROM installation

1. Allow your lab workstation to boot into Windows 9x.

2. Double-click the **My Computer** icon.

3. Verify that Windows 9x recognizes the CD-ROM drive.

4. Insert a CD-ROM disc into the drive.

5. Double-click the **CD-ROM drive** icon and verify that you can view the contents of the disc. If a CD-ROM icon doesn't appear in the My Computer window, follow the steps in "Installing an IDE CD-ROM driver in Windows 9x" below.

Installing an IDE CD-ROM driver in Windows 9x

Windows 9x normally detects a CD-ROM drive installation the first time it is booted with one installed. In the event that Windows 9x doesn't detect a CD-ROM drive, follow the steps below.

1. Click the **Start** button.

2. Point to **Settings** and click **Control Panel**.

3. Double-click the **Add New Hardware** icon.

4. Click the **Next** button three times to allow Windows to detect new hardware.

5. When the process is complete, allow Windows to install the proper device driver.

6. Reboot your lab workstation, and follow the steps in the section, "Testing an IDE CD-ROM installation."

Lab Notes

Using a CD-ROM drive—Note that most CD-ROM drives have an emergency eject hole, which can be used to eject a CD-ROM disc from the drive in the event of a mechanical failure.

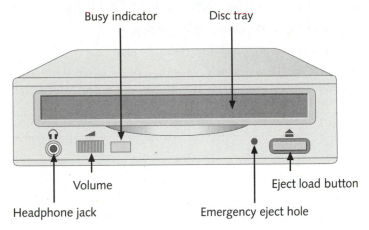

Figure 10-3 Front view of a typical CD-ROM drive

CERTIFICATION OBJECTIVES

Table 10-4 Core A+ Objectives

Objectives	Chapters	Page Numbers
1.2 Identify basic procedures for adding and removing field replaceable modules.	1, 3, 4, 11, 14	
B. Storage device	1, 14	11, 774-779
1.5 Identify proper procedures for installing and configuring IDE/EIDE devices.	6, 7	
A. Master/Slave	6, 7	282, 348-354
B. Devices per channel	6, 7	282, 348-354
1.7 Identify proper procedures for installing and configuring peripheral devices.	14, 15	
C. Storage devices	14	781, 782

Table 10-5 DOS/Windows A+ Objectives

Objectives	Chapters	Page Numbers
3.1 Identify the procedures for installing DOS, Windows 3.x, and Windows 95, and for bringing the software to a basic operational level.	6, 7, 12	
D. Loading drivers	12	611, 612
3.4 Identify procedures for loading/adding device drivers and the necessary software for certain devices.	4, 9, 10	
A. Windows 3.x procedures	4	198, 199
B. Windows 95 Plug and Play	9, 10	459-461, 526

10

Review Questions

Circle True or False.

1. All CD–ROM drives are installed into 3½-inch bays. True / False
2. An X32 CD–ROM drive is 32 times faster than an audio CD–ROM drive. True / False
3. The fastest CD–ROM drive that has ever been made is 32X. True / False
4. A computer can have only one CD–ROM drive. True / False
5. A standard CD–ROM drive has read-only capability. True / False
6. Laura has just installed a CD–ROM drive into her computer. Now when she powers on the system it doesn't boot properly. What is most likely the problem? Explain your answer.

_____

_____

_____

_____

_____

LAB 10.3 MULTIMEDIA SOUND

Objective

This lab exercise is designed to allow you to install and configure a sound card. After completing this lab exercise, you will be able to:

■ Install a sound card.

Materials Required

This lab exercise requires one complete lab workstation for every four students. The lab workstations should meet the following requirements:

■ 486 or better

■ 16MB of RAM

■ Windows 9x

One 8- or 16-bit sound card

One ESD mat

Grounding straps for each student

Documentation containing each sound card's jumper settings

Lab Setup & Safety Tips

■ Each lab workstation should have Windows 9x installed.

■ Verify that IRQ 5 and DMA 0 are available for use on all lab workstations.

■ Students must comply with standard ESD procedures.

■ Always unplug the power cord before touching any component within the case.

ACTIVITY

Installing a sound card

1. Power off the lab workstation.

2. Unplug the power cord.

3. Remove the case from the lab workstation.

4. Locate an available ISA slot for the sound card.

5. Remove the end-of-slot blank.

6. Using the provided documentation, verify that the sound card jumpers are configured to use IRQ 5 and DMA 0.

7. Gently slide the PCI expansion card into the PCI slot, moving the card from end to end until it is completely seated. *Warning*: Do not bend the card from side to side.

8. Mount the sound card.

9. Replace the case.

10. Plug in the power cord.

11. Click the **Start** button, point to **Settings**, and then click **Control Panel**.

12. Double-click the **Add New Hardware** icon.

13. Click the **Next** button three times and allow Windows 9x to detect your sound card.

14. When the process is complete, allow Windows to install the proper device driver.

If Windows does not detect the sound card

1. Click the **Start** button.

2. Point to **Settings** and click **Control Panel**.

3. Double-click the **Add New Hardware** icon.

4. Click the **Next** button twice.

5. Select the **No** option and then click the **Next** button.

6. Select the **Sound, video and game controller** option and then click the **Next** button.

7. Click the **Have Disk** button.

8. Insert the disk with the sound card drivers.

9. Click the **OK** button.

10. Select the sound card driver you want to use from the menu.

11. Click the **OK** button.

12. Click the **Next** button.

13. Click the **Finish** button.

14. Click the **Yes** button when you are prompted to restart your lab workstation.

Testing the sound card

1. Allow your lab workstation to boot into Windows 9x.

2. Verify that your speakers are properly plugged in and powered on.

3. Click the **Start** button and select **Run**.

4. Type **C:\WINDOWS\CHIMES.WAV** and press **Enter**.

5. If necessary, click the **play arrow**, which points to the right, to preview the sound.

Your workstation should respond by playing the chimes.wav file.

Lab Notes

What is a WAV file?—A WAV file is a sound file that is most commonly used to store multimedia sounds.

What is a MID file?—A MID, or MIDI, is a sound file that is most commonly used to store music.

What is the difference between an 8-bit and 16-bit sound card?—An 8-bit sound card uses 8 bits to store a sample value, and has a 256 sample size range. A 16-bit sound card uses 16 bits to store a sample value and has a sample size of up to 65,536.

A+ CERTIFICATION OBJECTIVES

Table 10-6 Core A+ Objectives

Objectives	Chapters	Page Numbers
1.3 Identify available IRQs, DMAs, and I/O addresses and procedures for configuring them for device installation.	2, 5, 7, 9	
A. Standard IRQ settings	2, 9	83, 90, 463
2.1 Identify common symptoms and problems associated with each module and how to troubleshoot and isolate the problems.	2, 3, 5, 7, 8, 10, 15, Appendices A and E	
E. Sound Card/Audio	10, Appendix E	543, E26

Review Questions

Circle True or False.

1. An 8-bit sound card produces a higher quality sound than a 16-bit sound card.
   True / False

2. All sound cards use a PCI bus. True / False

3. You can install a sound card's device driver by using the Add/Remove Programs icon in the Control Panel. True / False

4. To use a sound card you must have a set of speakers or headphones. True / False

5. Most sound cards include a built-in microphone and speakers. True / False

6. Jacob just installed a new sound card into his Windows 95 PC. Windows did not detect the sound card when he used the Add New Hardware option in the Control Panel. In the space below, describe to Jacob how to install the proper sound card driver.

_____

_____

_____

_____

_____

10

CHAPTER
11

ELECTRICITY AND POWER SUPPLIES

LABS INCLUDED IN THIS CHAPTER

♦ **LAB 11.1 AC ELECTRICITY**

♦ **LAB 11.2 DC ELECTRICITY**

♦ **LAB 11.3 POWER PROTECTION**

♦ **LAB 11.4 POWER CHAIN TROUBLESHOOTING**

LAB 11.1 AC ELECTRICITY

Objective

The objective of this lab exercise is to demonstrate and define some basic concepts and terminology related to the study and use of electricity. After completing this lab exercise, you will be able to:

- Create a simple switched circuit.
- Describe the relationship between voltage, amperage, ohms, and wattage.
- Use a multimeter to measure voltage and amperage.

Materials Required

For this lab exercise each group of four students will require the following materials:

- One 9-volt battery (AA is an acceptable substitute)
- One multimeter (capable of measuring amps)
- One DC light bulb
- One switch
- Three pieces of standard grade electrical wire
- Electrical tape to attach wires to the battery, if necessary

Lab Setup & Safety Tips

- Each group will require a clean desktop area for building their switched circuit.
- The instructor will teach each student how to configure the multimeter to measure volts and amps.

ACTIVITY

Creating a circuit

1. Attach one piece of wire to each lead on the light bulb.
2. Attach one of the wires to the battery's lead.
3. Attach the second wire to the other battery lead.
4. Observe the results.

5. In the space provided below, draw a diagram demonstrating the flow of electricity in the circuit you have created. Be sure to note the direction of the current's flow.

Adding a switch

1. Disconnect the wire from the negative side of the battery.

2. Attach the wire to an available lead on the switch.

3. Attach the third wire to the other switch lead and then attach it to the battery.

4. Observe how the switch manages the circuit.

Measuring voltage

1. Configure your multimeter to measure the voltage of your circuit.

2. Attach the +/- leads from your multimeter to the respective +/- sides of the light bulb.

3. Be sure that the switch is turned to the ON position.

4. Record the voltage of your circuit: _____

Measuring amps

1. Configure your multimeter to measure the amps of your circuit.

2. Disconnect the wire that is not currently attached to the switch.

3. Attach the respective +/- side of the multimeter to the battery lead that is not attached to any wires.

4. Attach the respective +/- side of the multimeter to the light bulb that is not attached to any wires.

5. Turn the switch to the ON position.

6. Record the amps found in your circuit: _____

11

Lab Notes

What does AC mean?—Alternating current (AC) is current that cycles back and forth rather than traveling in only one direction. Normally between 110 and 115 AC volts are supplied from a standard wall outlet.

What are amps?—Amps are units of measurement for electrical current. One volt across a resistance of one ohm will produce a flow of one amp.

What are volts?—A volt is a measure of electrical pressure differential. A computer power supply usually provides four separate voltages: +12 V, −12 V, +5 V and −5 V.

What is wattage?—Wattage is a measure of the total amount of power that is needed to operate an electrical device.

What are ohms?— An ohm is the standard unit of measurement for electrical resistance. Resistors are rated in ohms.

Review Questions

Circle True or False.

1. Resistance is measured in ohms. True / False

2. A switch can act as a break in a circuit. True / False

3. AC is an acronym for ampere. True / False

4. A multimeter can be used only to measure voltage. True / False

5. In a circuit, amps and volts are always the same amount when measured. True / False

6. Describe the difference in multimeter placement for measuring volts and amps.

_____

_____

_____

_____

_____

LAB 11.2 DC ELECTRICITY

Objective

The objective of this lab exercise is to familiarize you with the different functions of a PC's power supply. After completing this lab exercise, you will be able to:

- Describe the function of a PC power supply.
- Use a multimeter to test and measure the power supply output of a PC.
- Successfully troubleshoot power supply issues.

Materials Required

This lab exercise requires one complete lab workstation for every four students. The lab workstation should meet the following requirements:

- 486 or better
- 16MB of RAM
- Windows 9x

One multimeter

Tools necessary to remove the lab workstation's case and power supply

Lab Setup & Safety Tips

- Each lab workstation should be in good working order.
- Students should always follow proper ESD procedures when working with computer components.
- For the purpose of this lab exercise the systemboard power connectors will be referred to as the P8 and P9 connectors.
- If students are working in pairs, identify one as Student 1 and the other as Student 2.

ACTIVITY

Measuring the +12V DC wire of a PC's power supply

1. Unplug your lab workstation.
2. Configure your multimeter to measure voltages within the following range: −5V DC/+15V DC.
3. Remove the case.
4. Using Figure 11-1 for reference, attach the respective multimeter leads to the ground and +12V wires (connect the multimeter to the power supply connector outside the case on a flat surface that can be easily seen and controlled).

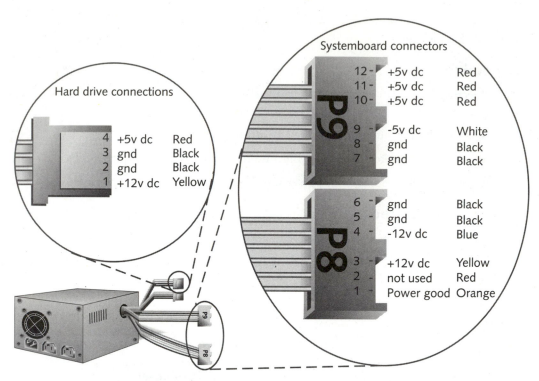

Figure 11-1 Power supply connections

5. Before plugging in the PC, verify that no other metal pieces are touching the systemboard or power supply, which could cause a short.

6. Plug in the power cord.

7. Stand clear of the lab workstation and power it on.

8. Record the results displayed on the multimeter: _____

9. Refer to the table below to verify that the recorded voltage falls within the acceptable range.

10. Power off your lab workstation.

Table 11-1 Twelve leads to the systemboard from the power supply

Connection	Lead	Description	Acceptable Range
P8	1	"Power Good"	
	2	Not used	
	3	+12 volts	+8.5 to +12.6 volts
	4	−12 volts	−8.5 to −12.6 volts
	5	Black ground	
	6	Black ground	
P9	7	Black ground	
	8	Black ground	
	9	−5 volts	−4.5 to −5.4 volts
	10	+5 volts	+2.4 to +5.2 volts
	11	+5 volts	+2.4 to +5.2 volts
	12	+5 volts	+2.4 to +5.2 volts

Measuring the +15 V DC wire of a PC's power supply

1. Unplug your lab workstation.
2. Configure your multimeter to measure voltages within the following range: −5V DC/+15V DC.
3. Using Figure 11-1, attach the respective multimeter leads to the ground and +15 V DC wires (connect the multimeter to the power supply connector outside the case on a flat surface that can be easily seen and controlled).
4. Before plugging in the PC, verify that no other metal pieces or objects are touching the systemboard or power supply, which could cause a short.
5. Plug in the power cord.
6. Stand clear of the lab workstation and power it on.
7. Record the results displayed on the multimeter: _____
8. Refer to the table from the previous activity to verify that the recorded voltage falls within the acceptable range.
9. Power off your lab workstation.

Measuring the +5 V DC wire of the P9 systemboard power connector

1. Unplug your lab workstation.
2. Configure your multimeter to measure voltages within the following range: −5V DC/+15 V DC.
3. Using Figure 11-1, attach the respective multimeter leads to the ground and +5 V DC wires (connect the multimeter to the power supply connector outside the case on a flat surface that can be easily seen and controlled).
4. Before plugging in the PC, verify that no other metal pieces or objects are touching the systemboard or power supply, which could cause a short.
5. Plug in the power cord.
6. Stand clear of the lab workstation and power it on.
7. Record the results displayed on the multimeter: _____
8. Refer to the table from the first exercise to verify that the recorded voltage falls within the acceptable range.
9. Power off the computer.

Measuring the +12 V DC wire of the P8 systemboard power connector

1. Unplug your lab workstation.
2. Configure your multimeter to measure voltages within the following range: −5VDC/+15 V DC
3. Using Figure 11-1, attach the respective multimeter leads to the ground and +12V DC wires (connect the multimeter to the power supply connector outside the case on a flat surface that can be easily seen and controlled).
4. Before plugging in the PC, verify that no other metal pieces or objects are touching the systemboard or power supply, which could cause a short.
5. Plug in the power cord.
6. Stand clear of the lab workstation and power it on.
7. Record the results displayed on the multimeter: _____
8. Refer to the table from the first exercise to verify that the recorded voltage falls within the acceptable range.
9. Power off the computer.

11

Removing a power supply
Student 1

1. Unplug your lab workstation.
2. Unplug all of the power connectors.
3. Locate the mounting screws of the power supply.
4. Unscrew and dismount the power supply.
5. Give the power supply and mounting screws to Student 2.

Installing a power supply
Student 2

1. Place the power supply into the mounting position.
2. After verifying that the power supply is properly aligned, screw the screws into place.
3. Attach each of the power connectors to their respective devices.
4. Plug in the power cord.
5. Stand clear of the lab workstation and power it on. Verify that all of the devices are functioning properly.

Lab Notes

Are power connectors for SCSI devices different from those for IDE devices?—No, the power connectors generally used for SCSI devices provide the same functionality as they would for an IDE device.

CERTIFICATION OBJECTIVES

Table 11-2   Core A+ Objectives

Objectives	Chapters	Page Numbers
1.1 Identify basic terms, concepts, and functions of system modules, including how each module should work during normal operation.	1, 2, 11, 15	
B. Power supply	1, 11	19
1.2 Identify basic procedures for adding and removing field replaceable modules.	1, 3, 4, 11, 14	
C. Power supply	1, 11, 14	19, 575, 576, 766-771
2.1 Identify common symptoms and problems associated with each module and how to troubleshoot and isolate the problems.	2, 3, 5, 7, 8, 10, 15, Appendices A and E	
K. Power supply	8, 11, Appendix E	422, 423, 565, 566, 573-575, E7
O. Troubleshooting tools, e.g., multimeter	8, 11	409, 410, 566-568
3.2 Identify procedures and devices for protecting against environmental hazard.	11, 18	
B. Determining the signs of power issues	11	573-575
3.3 Identify the potential hazards and proper safety procedures relating to lasers and high-voltage equipment.	11, 18	
B. High-voltage equipment	11	573
C. Power supply	11	573

Review Questions

Circle True or False.

1. A hard drive connector's red wire should have a voltage that falls within the range of −15V DC to +15V DC. True / False

2. The P8 and P9 connectors are designed to be used for SCSI devices. True / False

3. Removing a power supply is as simple as removing the power connectors and dismounting the power supply. True / False

4. The ground wire should have a voltage reading that falls within the ranges of −5V DC to −15V DC. True / False

5. The power supply is normally mounted to the systemboard. True / False

6. Ginger's PC keeps rebooting by itself. She suspects that the power supply is faulty. In the space below, describe why Ginger's suspicion is or is not a realistic possibility.

   _____

   _____

   _____

   _____

   _____

7. John tested one of his power supply connectors by attaching his multimeter's leads to the two center wires of a hard drive connector with the system powered on. He received a reading of 0 volts. He believes that he will need to replace the power supply. In the space below, describe why John should or should not replace the power supply.

   _____

   _____

   _____

   _____

   _____

11

LAB 11.3 POWER PROTECTION

Objective

The objective of this lab exercise is to allow you install and configure a surge protector and an uninterruptible power supply (UPS) device. After completing this lab exercise, you will be able to:

- Describe the functionality of a surge protector.
- Properly install and configure a surge protector.
- Describe the functionality of a UPS device.
- Properly install and configure a UPS device.
- Properly install and configure a power conditioner.

Materials Required

This lab exercise requires one complete lab workstation for every four students. The lab workstations should meet the following requirements:

- 486 or better
- 16MB of RAM
- Windows 9x

One surge protector

One UPS device of any type

One power conditioner

Lab Setup & Safety Tips

- Each lab workstation should have Windows 9x installed and functioning properly.
- Students should always follow proper ESD procedures when working with computer components.

ACTIVITY

Installing a surge protector

1. Power off your lab workstation.
2. Power off your monitor and any other peripheral devices.
3. Plug the provided surge protector into the wall outlet.
4. Plug each of your peripheral devices into the surge protector (this includes the system unit and monitor).
5. Power on the surge protector.
6. Power on your lab workstation.
7. Power on your monitor and other peripheral devices (this includes the system unit and monitor).
8. Verify that your PC is functioning properly.

Installing a UPS device

1. Power off your system unit.
2. Power off any additional peripherals that you want to be protected by the UPS device.

3. Unplug the system unit and the peripheral devices.

4. Plug the UPS device into the wall outlet.

5. Plug the system unit into the UPS device.

6. Plug the additional peripheral devices into the UPS.

7. Power on the UPS device.

8. Power on the system unit and additionally protected peripherals.

9. Verify that the system unit and each additionally protected device are functioning properly.

Observing the functionality of a UPS device

1. Power on your system unit and allow it to boot into Windows 9x.

2. Power on your additional peripheral devices.

3. Unplug the UPS device.

4. Record the results.

_____

_____

_____

_____

_____

Installing a power conditioner

1. Power off your system unit.

2. Power off any additional peripherals you want to be protected by the power conditioner.

3. Unplug the system unit and the peripheral devices.

4. Plug the provided power conditioner into the wall outlet.

5. Plug the system unit into the power conditioner.

6. Plug the additional peripheral devices into the power conditioner.

7. Power on the system unit and additionally protected peripherals.

8. Verify that the system unit and each additionally protected device are functioning properly.

Lab Notes

What is an in-line UPS?—An in-line UPS is a device that continuously provides power through a battery-powered circuit. Because it requires no switching, it ensures continuous power to the user.

What is a standby UPS?—A standby UPS is a device that quickly switches from an AC power source to a battery-powered source during a brownout or power outage.

What is an intelligent UPS?—An intelligent UPS is connected to a computer by way of a serial cable so that software on the computer can monitor and control the UPS.

What is a power conditioner?—A power conditioner is a device that regulates, or conditions, the power, providing continuous voltage during brownouts.

CERTIFICATION OBJECTIVES

Table 11-3 Core A+ Objectives

Objectives	Chapters	Page Numbers
3.2 Identify procedures and devices for protecting against environmental hazard.	11, 18	
A. UPS (uninterruptible power supply) and suppressors	11	580, 583-586
C. Proper methods of storage of components for future use	18	978, 979

Review Questions

Circle True or False.

1. All UPS devices provide the same functionality. True / False

2. A power conditioner will provide battery power for five minutes in the case of an outage. True / False

3. Surge protectors eventually deteriorate. True / False

4. An intelligent UPS can be controlled by software. True / False

5. Describe how a surge protector provides protection from power spikes.

_____

_____

_____

_____

_____

6. You are employed as a network administrator at Pictures, Inc. Your employer has asked you to assess the need for UPS devices for each of their 10 servers. After talking with the staff you learn that 7 of the servers are used for e-mail and bulletin board communications. The other 3 servers are used to maintain all of the company's accounting inventory databases. Pictures, Inc. has asked that you provide two proposals for them, the first outlining the ideal protection plan, and the other outlining the minimum protection requirements.

Power Protection Plan A (ideal)

_____

_____

_____

_____

_____

Power Protection Plan B (minimum requirement)

_____

_____

_____

_____

_____

LAB 11.4 POWER CHAIN TROUBLESHOOTING

Objective

The objective of this lab exercise is to develop your electrical troubleshooting skills. After completing this lab exercise, you will be able to:

- Identify a power issue.

- Repair an electrical problem.

- Describe some common symptoms of electrical problems.

Materials Required

This lab exercise requires one complete lab workstation for every four students. The lab workstations should meet the following requirements:

- 486 or better

- 16MB of RAM

- Windows 9x

Tools necessary to remove the lab workstation's case.

Lab Setup & Safety Tips

- Each lab workstation should have Windows 9x installed and functioning properly.

- Students should always follow proper ESD procedures when working with computer components.

- If students are working in pairs, identify one as Student 1 and the other as Student 2.

ACTIVITY

Troubleshooting a power supply

Student 1

The following should be completed while Student 2 is away from the lab workstation:

1. Power off your lab workstation.

2. Unplug the power cord.

3. Remove the case.

4. Unplug the P8 connector from the systemboard.

5. Replace the case.

6. Plug in the power cord.

7. Power on the lab workstation.

Student 2

After Student 1 has reconfigured the lab workstation, answer the following questions, and then repair the lab workstation:

1. Are there any error messages? If so, write them down:

   _____

   _____

   _____

   _____

   _____

2. What is the problem? Be specific.

   _____

   _____

   _____

   _____

   _____

3. List several possible solutions:

   _____

   _____

   _____

   _____

   _____

4. Test your theory (solution) and record the results:

   _____

   _____

   _____

   _____

   _____

5. How did you discover the problem?

   _____

   _____

   _____

   _____

   _____

6. In the future, what would you do differently to improve your troubleshooting process?

   _____

   _____

   _____

   _____

Student 2

The following should be completed while Student 1 is away from the lab workstation:

1. Power off your lab workstation.

2. Unplug the power cord.

3. Remove the case.

4. Reverse the P8 and P9 power connectors.

5. Replace the case.

6. Plug in the power cord.

7. Power on the lab workstation.

Student 1

After Student 2 has reconfigured the lab workstation, answer the following questions and repair the lab workstation:

1. Are there any error messages? If so, write them down:

   _____

   _____

   _____

   _____

   _____

2. What is the problem? Be specific.

   _____

   _____

   _____

   _____

   _____

3. List several possible solutions:

   _____

   _____

   _____

   _____

   _____

4. Test your theory (solution) and record the results:

   _____

   _____

   _____

   _____

   _____

11

5. How did you discover the problem?

_____

_____

_____

_____

_____

6. In the future, what would you do differently to improve your troubleshooting process?

_____

_____

_____

_____

_____

Lab Notes

How should I repair a power supply that is shorting?—As a PC technician you should *never* open or attempt to repair the internal working of a power supply. Your job is to diagnose the problem and replace the power supply, if necessary.

An electrical troubleshooting tip—When troubleshooting electricity, mentally follow the path the electricity follows, starting from the wall outlet and working your way through the entire PC. In this way it quickly becomes obvious which part of a PC is having a power problem and, more importantly, which device is causing the electrical problem.

CERTIFICATION OBJECTIVES

Table 11-4   Core A+ Objectives

Objectives		Chapters	Page Numbers
1.1	Identify basic terms, concepts, and functions of system modules, including how each module should work during normal operation.	1, 2, 11, 15	
B.	Power supply	1, 11	19, 565, 566, 573
3.2	Identify procedures and devices for protecting against environmental hazard.	11, 18	
B.	Determining the signs of power issues	11	573-575

Review Questions

Circle **True** or **False**.

1. If a power supply's fan does not spin, it could indicate that the power supply has failed. **True / False**

2. The P8 and P9 power connectors can be attached to the systemboard in any order. **True / False**

3. Hard drive connectors and the systemboard connector use the same voltage. **True / False**

4. A common mistake is to attach the hard drive power connector to the systemboard. **True / False**

5. What should be the voltage of a power supply's ground wires?

_____

_____

_____

_____

6. Elliot has just replaced his systemboard, and now his computer won't boot. List three possible power-related problems that could be wrong with his system.

_____

_____

_____

_____

_____

11

12

SUPPORTING WINDOWS 3.x AND WINDOWS 95

LABS INCLUDED IN THIS CHAPTER

♦ **LAB 12.1** INSTALLING WINDOWS 3.1

♦ **LAB 12.2** CUSTOMIZING WINDOWS 3.x

♦ **LAB 12.3** INSTALLING WINDOWS 95

♦ **LAB 12.4** CUSTOMIZING WINDOWS 95

♦ **LAB 12.5** INSTALLING WINDOWS 98

LAB 12.1 INSTALLING WINDOWS 3.1

Objective

The objective of this lab exercise is to install Windows 3.1. After completing this lab exercise, you will be able to:

- Install Windows 3.1.
- Describe the Windows 3.1 installation process.
- Locate and describe the function of Windows 3.1 system files.

Materials Required

This lab exercise requires one complete lab workstation for every four students. The lab workstation should meet the following requirements:

- 486 or better
- 8MB of RAM
- Window 3.1 installation files

One DOS system disk

Lab Setup & Safety Tips

- Each lab workstation should be preloaded with the Windows 3.1 installation files, which should be placed in a directory named C:\WIN3.1.

ACTIVITY

Installing Windows 3.1

1. Insert the system disk into drive A.

2. Power on your lab workstation and allow it to boot from the DOS system disk.

3. At the C prompt, type **CD C:\WIN3.1** and press **Enter**.

4. Type **SETUP** and press **Enter**. Your lab workstation should respond by beginning the Windows 3.1 installation.

5. Press **Enter**.

6. Press **Enter** to select the Express Setup option.

7. Press the **Backspace** key to clear the Windows system directory path.

8. Type **C:\WINDOWS3.1** and press **Enter**.

9. Type your name and press **Enter**.

10. Press **Enter**.

11. Click the **Cancel** button to skip the printer driver installation.

12. Click the **Skip Tutorial** button.

13. Click the **Restart Computer** button.

Identifying Windows 3.1 system files

1. Using your lab workstation and textbook for reference, write the path of the following system files and describe their functionality.

   a. WIN.INI

   _____

   _____

   _____

   _____

   _____

   b. SYSTEM.INI

   _____

   _____

   _____

   _____

   _____

   c. USER.EXE

   _____

   _____

   _____

   _____

   _____

   d. GDI.EXE

   _____

   _____

   _____

   _____

   _____

   e. WIN.COM

   _____

   _____

   _____

   _____

   _____

12

f. KRNLXXX.EXE

_____

_____

_____

_____

_____

g. PROGMAN.EXE

_____

_____

_____

_____

_____

h. PROGMAN.INI

_____

_____

_____

_____

_____

Lab Notes

Express Setup—Express Setup allows Windows 3.1 to automatically install a group of preselected operating system components.

Custom Setup—Custom Setup allows you to select the components that you want to install.

Reinstalling Windows—This option, sometimes referred to as upgrading Windows, allows you to install Windows 3.1 over the currently installed version. You can use this option to repair a damaged installation of Windows 3.1.

What should I do if the setup program stops?—If the setup program stops, it is most likely having problems detecting one or more of your hardware devices. To skip the detection process, reboot the PC and restart the Setup program using the following command: C:\WIN3.1\SETUP /I.

What is a (GPF) General Protection Fault?—General Protection Faults (GPFs) were originally error messages that indicated an application was misusing memory or attempting to write to a memory area that wasn't allocated to it. As the use of Windows 3.1 has become more prevalent, a GPF has come to mean that an application error of some kind has occurred.

What does the error message "Invalid Working Directory" mean?—The Invalid Working Directory error message indicates that the program path has not been properly defined for application execution.

A+ CERTIFICATION OBJECTIVES

Table 12-1 DOS/Windows A+ Objectives

Objectives	Chapters	Page Numbers
1.1 Identify the operating system's functions, structure, and major system files.	1, 2, 4, 12, Appendices C and E	
A. Functions of DOS, Windows 3.x and Windows 95.	1, 2	35, 74
B. Major components of DOS, Windows 3.x and Windows 95.	1, 2	35, 75, 76
C. Contrasts between Windows 3.x and Windows 95.	1, 12	36, 624-630
D. Major system files: what they are, where they are located, how they are used and what they contain:	2, 4, 12	74-77, 188, 198-200, 598-600
1. System, Configuration, and User Interface files	2, 4, 12	74-77, 188, 198-200, 598-600
b. Windows 3.x		
1. Win.ini	2, 12	79, 77, 602-608
2. System.ini	2, 12	77, 598, 602-608
3. User.exe	12	598-600
4. Gdi.exe	12	598-600
5. Win.com	2	76, 77
6. Progman.ini	2, 12	77, 600, 602-608
7. progMAN.exe	12	600
8. Krnlxxx.exe	12	600
1.2 Identify ways to navigate the operating system and how to get to needed technical information.	1, 12	
B. Procedures for navigating through the Windows 3.x/Windows 95 operating system, accessing, and retrieving information.	1, 12	49, 50, 600, 601
2.2 Identify typical memory conflict problems and how to optimize memory use.	4, 12	
A. What a memory conflict is	12	620-622
B. How it happens	12	620-622
C. When to employ utilities	12	620-622
E. General Protection Fault	12	620-622
3.1 Identify the procedures for installing DOS, Windows 3.x, and Windows 95, and for bringing the software to a basic operational level.	6, 7, 12	
C. Run appropriate set up utility	7, 12	362, 637, 638
D. Loading drivers	12	611, 612
4.3 Recognize common problems and determine how to resolve them.	1, 4, 5, 8, 12, 16, Appendix E	
A. Common problems		
1. General Protection Fault	8, 12	427, 428, 620
3. Invalid working directory		
4. System lock up	1	47, 48
5. Option will not function	8	427, 428
6. Application will not start or load	8	427, 428

12

Review Questions

Circle True or False.

1. To install Windows 3.1 you must run the install program. True / False

2. The GPF or General Protection Fault indicates that an application error has occurred, possibly due to the misuse of memory. True / False

3. The WIN.INI stores the setting for the Windows 3.1 swap file. True / False

4. Choosing the Custom Setup option during the Windows 3.1 installation process allows you to choose the Windows 3.1 components you want to install. True / False

5. Windows 3.1 must always be installed in a directory named Windows. True / False

6. The SYSTEM.INI stores Windows 3.1 application configuration data. True / False

7. Lily wants to install Windows 3.1 on her laptop. She copied the installation files to her hard drive and ran the Setup program. The Windows Setup program is now asking her whether she wants to use Express Setup or Custom Setup. She asks you to describe the difference to her because she doesn't want to make the wrong choice. Write your answer to Lily below:

_____

_____

_____

_____

_____

LAB 12.2 CUSTOMIZING WINDOWS 3.X

Objective

This lab exercise is designed to enable you to configure some common settings in the Windows 3.x environment. After completing this lab exercise, you will be able to:

- Properly configure Windows 3.x to use a screen saver, desktop wallpaper, and customized groups.
- Describe how the Startup group is used in the Windows 3.x environment.

Materials Required

This lab exercise requires one complete lab workstation for every four students. The lab workstations should meet the following requirements:

- 486 or better
- 8MB of RAM
- Windows 3.x

Lab Setup & Safety Tips

- Each lab workstation should have Windows 3.x installed and functioning properly.

ACTIVITY

Configuring your desktop wallpaper in the Windows 3.x environment

1. Power on your lab workstation and allow it to boot into Windows 3.x.
2. Open the **Program Manager** window.
3. Double-click the **Main** group icon.
4. Double-click the **Control Panel** icon.
5. Double-click the **Desktop** icon.
6. Click the **Wallpaper** list arrow, and then click **zigzag.bmp**.
7. Click the **OK** button. Your lab workstation should respond by displaying a zigzag pattern behind the Program Manager window.

Configuring your screen saver in the Windows 3.x environment

1. Power on your lab workstation and allow it to boot into Windows 3.x.
2. Open the **Program Manager** window.
3. Double-click the **Main** group icon.
4. Double-click the **Control Panel** icon.
5. Double-click the **Desktop** icon.
6. Click the **Screen Saver** list arrow, and then click **Mystify** or the screen saver of your choice.
7. Click the **OK** button. Your lab workstation should respond by displaying the Mystify screen saver after the screen saver time period has elapsed.

12

Creating a personalized program group

1. Power on your lab workstation and allow it to boot into Windows 3.x.

2. Open the **Program Manager** window.

3. Click the **File** menu.

4. Select **New**.

5. Click the **Program Group** option button.

6. Click the **OK** button.

7. Type **MY GROUP** in the Description box.

8. Type **MY GROUP** in the Group File box.

9. Click the **OK** button.

10. Locate your new group in the Program Manager window, and then double-click it.

Using the Startup group

Use the Startup group to configure your operating system to automatically start one or more programs after the operating system has completed initialization. To start a program automatically, complete the following steps:

1. Power on your lab workstation and allow it to boot into Windows 3.x.

2. Open the **Program Manager** window.

3. Double-click the **Startup** group icon.

4. Double-click the **Accessories** group icon.

5. Drag the **Notepad** icon from the **Accessories** group to the **Startup** group.

6. Close the **Startup** group and the **Accessories** group.

7. Click the **File** menu in the Program Manager window.

8. Click **Exit Windows**.

9. Click **OK** in the confirmation message box.

10. At the C prompt, type **WIN**.

11. When Windows has restarted, notice that the Notepad program now starts after the operating system has been initialized.

Lab Notes

DOS commands and Windows 3.x utilities

MSD—MSD stands for Microsoft System Diagnostics; this utility was originally designed to help you identify and resolve resource conflicts in the DOS environment.

MEM—The MEM command is used to view how memory is being allocated in the DOS environment.

SCANDISK—The SCANDISK utility is designed to check the FAT for cross-linked files and other inconsistencies, and to repair them, if necessary.

DEFRAG—The DEFRAG utility is used to reorganize clusters on your hard drive and improve disk performance.

SYSEDIT—SYSEDIT is used in the Windows environment and allows you to view and make changes to all of the most commonly used configuration files, such as the AUTOEXEC.BAT, CONFIG.SYS, WIN.INI, and SYSTEM.INI.

Where can I get more information about Windows 3.x?—You can purchase a Windows 3.x user's manual, but it is easier and more cost-effective to read the documentation included with the operating system. The following five files are located in the Windows directory:

Readme.wri

Printers.wri

Networks.wri

Sysini.wri

Winini.wri

12

A+ CERTIFICATION OBJECTIVES

Table 12-2   DOS/Windows A+ Objectives

Objectives	Chapters	Page Numbers
1.2 Identify ways to navigate the operating system and how to get to needed technical information.	1, 12	
B. Procedures for navigating through the Windows 3.x/Windows 95 operating system, accessing, and retrieving information.	1, 12	119, 510, 600, 601
1.4 Identify the procedures for basic disk management.	5, 6, 7, 18 Appendix F	
A. Using disk management utilities	6	320-322
E. Defragmenting	6	320-322
F. ScanDisk	6	322
4.3 Recognize common problems and determine how to resolve them	1, 4, 5, 8, 16, Appendix E	
B. **DOS and Windows-based utilities**		
1. ScanDisk	8	411
5. Defrag.exe	8	411
8. MSD.EXE	5	260
9. Mem.exe	4	205-207
10. SYSEDIT.EXE	12	603

Review Questions

Circle True or False.

1. You can configure your desktop wallpaper by using the Accessories group. True / False

2. The term "desktop wallpaper" refers to the .BMP file displayed as the background on your computer screen. True / False

3. You cannot create additional groups in the Program Manager window. True / False

4. You can configure Windows 3.x to automatically start applications. True / False

5. You can configure a screen saver by using the Control Panel Desktop icon. True / False

6. Alice wants to create a program group containing all of her most commonly used applications. Describe below how Alice could accomplish this task.

_____

_____

_____

_____

_____

LAB 12.3 INSTALLING WINDOWS 95

Objective

The objective of this lab exercise is for you to install the Windows 95 operating system. After completing this lab exercise, you will be able to:

- Install Windows 95.
- Accurately describe the Windows 95 installation process.
- Locate and describe the function of Windows 95 system files.

Materials Required

This lab exercise requires one complete lab workstation for every four students. The lab workstations should meet the following requirements:

- 486 or better
- 16MB of RAM
- Windows 95 installation files

One DOS system disk

One blank, formatted disk

A valid Windows 95 product ID for each lab workstation

Lab Setup & Safety Tips

- Each lab workstation should be preloaded with the Windows 95 installation files, which should be placed in a directory named C:\WIN95.

ACTIVITY

Installing Windows 95

1. Insert the system disk into drive A.
2. Power on your lab workstation and allow it to boot from the DOS system disk.
3. At the C prompt, type **CD C:\WIN95** and press **Enter**.
4. Type **SETUP** and press **Enter**.
5. Press **Enter** to allow the Setup program to run the SCANDISK utility.
6. Click the **Continue** button.
7. Click the **Yes** button.
8. Click the **Next** button.
9. Select the **Other Directory** option and click the **Next** button.
10. Type **C:\WINDOWS.95** and click the **Next** button.
11. In the Setup Option window, click the **Typical** option and then click the **Next** button.
12. Type the product ID provided by your instructor.
13. Type your name.
14. Click the **Next** button.
15. Select the hardware components installed on your lab workstation, and click the **Next** button.

12

16. Click the **Next** button to accept the defaults on the next three windows.

17. Insert your blank floppy disk into drive A.

18. Click the **OK** button.

19. Remove the floppy disk and click the **OK** button.

20. Click the **Finish** button.

21. Select the proper time zone, and click the **OK** button.

22. Click the **Cancel** button when prompted to install a printer driver.

23. Click the **OK** button to restart the computer.

Identifying Windows 95 system files

1. Using your lab workstation and textbook for reference, write the path of the following system files and describe their functionality.

    a. IO.SYS

_____

_____

_____

_____

_____

    b. MSDOS.SYS

_____

_____

_____

_____

_____

    c. COMMAND.COM

_____

_____

_____

_____

_____

    d. WIN.INI

_____

_____

_____

_____

_____

e. PROGMAN.INI

_____

_____

_____

_____

f. SYSTEM.DAT

_____

_____

_____

_____

g. USER.DAT

_____

_____

_____

_____

12

Lab Notes

What do I do if the Setup program stops?—If the Windows 95 Setup program stops during the installation, you restart it by simply rebooting the PC and running the Setup program again. Unlike Windows 3.x however, Windows 95 has the ability to learn from its mistakes. For example, if Windows 95 crashes during the installation process, when you restart, the setup program automatically skips the process that hung the system during the previous installation attempt.

Express Setup—Express Setup allows Windows 95 to automatically install a group of preselected operating system components.

Custom Setup—Custom Setup allows you to select the components that you want to install.

Reinstalling Windows—This option, sometimes referred to as upgrading Windows, allows you to install Windows 95 over the currently installed version. You can use this option to repair a damaged installation of Windows 95.

A+ CERTIFICATION OBJECTIVES

Table 12-3   DOS/Windows A+ Objectives

Objectives	Chapters	Page Numbers
1.1 Identify the operating system's functions, structure, and major system files.	1, 2, 3, 4, 12, Appendices C and E	
A. Functions of DOS, Windows 3.x and Windows 95.	1, 2	35, 74
B. Major components of DOS, Windows 3.x and Windows 95.	1, 2	35, 75, 76
C. Contrasts between Windows 3.x and Windows 95.	1, 12	36, 624-630
D. Major system files: what they are, where they are located, how they are used and what they contain:	2, 4, 12	74-77,188, 198-200 598-600
c. Windows 95		
1. Io.sys	2	74
2. Msdos.sys	2	75
3. Command.com	2	74
5. System.dat	12	650
6. User.dat	12	650
3.1 Identify the procedures for installing DOS, Windows 3.x, and Windows 95, and for bringing the software to a basic operational level.	6, 7, 12	
C. Run appropriate set up utility	7, 12	362, 637, 638
D. Loading drivers	12	611, 612
3.2 Identify steps to perform an operating system upgrade.	12	
A. Upgrading from DOS to Windows 95.	12	637, 638
B. Upgrading from Windows 3.x to Windows 95.	12	637, 638, 641
3.3 Identify the basic system boot sequences, and alternative ways to boot the system software, including the steps to create an emergency boot disk with utilities installed.	2, 5, 7, 8, 12, Appendix E	
A. Files required to boot	2, 5	72, 261
B. Creating emergency boot disk	2, 5	103, 259-262

Review Questions

Circle True or False.

1. Windows 3.x and Windows 95 use the same Setup program. True / False

2. During the Windows 95 installation, you are given the option to install MSN connectivity. True / False

3. The Windows 95 Setup program launches the SCANDISK utility before installing or upgrading the operating system. True / False

4. During the Windows 95 installation, you can create an emergency repair disk. True / False

5. What are the filenames of the SYSTEM.DAT and the USER.DAT backup files that are created automatically by Windows 95?

_____

_____

_____

_____

_____

6. If you were installing Windows 95 on a laptop, which of the following component packages would be ideal, and why would or wouldn't they?

Typical

Custom

Portable

_____

_____

_____

_____

_____

12

Lab 12.4 Customizing Windows 95

Objective

This lab exercise allows you to configure some common settings in the Windows 95 environment. After completing this lab exercise, you will be able to:

- Properly configure Windows 95 to use a screen saver, desktop wallpaper, and customized shortcuts.
- Modify the Start menu.
- Install a printer driver in the Windows 95 environment.

Materials Required

This lab exercise requires one complete lab workstation for every four students. The lab workstations should meet the following requirements:

- 486 or better
- 16MB of RAM
- Windows 95

Lab Setup & Safety Tips

- Each lab workstation should have Windows 95 installed and functioning properly.

Activity

Configuring your desktop wallpaper in Windows 95

1. Power on your lab workstation and allow it to boot into Windows 95.
2. Right-click the desktop, and then click **Properties** on the shortcut menu.
3. In the **Wallpaper** list box, click the **Clouds** wallpaper or the wallpaper of your choice.
4. Click the **Apply** button.
5. Click the **OK** button.

Configuring your screen saver in Windows 95

1. Power on your lab workstation and allow it to boot into Windows 95.
2. Right-click the desktop, and then click **Properties** on the shortcut menu.
4. Click the **Screen Saver** tab.
5. Click the **Screen Saver** list arrow.
6. Click **Mystify** or the screen saver of your choice.
7. Click the **Apply** button.
8. Click the **OK** button.

Creating personalized program shortcuts

1. Right-click the desktop, and then point to **New** on the shortcut menu.
2. Click **Shortcut**.
3. Type **C:\WINDOWS.95\WINFILE.EXE** and press **Enter**.

4. In the Select a name for the shortcut box, type **File Manager**.

5. Click the **Finish** button.

Customizing your Start menu

1. Right-click the taskbar.

2. Select **Properties** from the shortcut menu as shown in Figure 12-1.

Figure 12-1   Windows 95 taskbar shortcut menu

3. Click the **Start Menu Programs** tab.

4. Click the **Add** button to see the Taskbar Properties dialog box, illustrated in Figure 12-2.

Figure 12-2   Taskbar Properties dialog box

5. Type **C:\WINDOWS.95\WINFILE.EXE**.

6. Click the **Next** button.

7. Double-click the **Accessories** folder.

8. In the Select a name for the shortcut box, type **File Manager**.

9. Click the **Finish** button.

10. Click the **OK** button.

11. Verify that the shortcut was properly added to the Accessories group by clicking the **Start** button, pointing to **Programs**, and then pointing to **Accessories**.

12. Click the newly created **File Manager** shortcut.

Installing a printer driver

1. Power on your lab workstation and allow it to boot into Windows 95.

2. Double-click the **My Computer** icon.

3. Double-click the **Printers** folder.

4. Double-click **Add Printer**.

5. Click the **Next** button.

6. Choose the **My computer** option, and click the **Next** button.

7. Choose the correct printer driver by selecting the appropriate manufacturer and printer model, and then click the **Next** button.

8. Select the appropriate printer port, and click the **Next** button.

9. Click the **Next** button again to use the default printer name.

10. Click the **Finish** button to complete the printer driver installation.

Lab Notes

What is Safe Mode?—Safe Mode is a way of starting Windows 95 with a minimum amount of Windows drivers. Note that Safe Mode is designed to be used for troubleshooting only.

What is DOS Mode?—Like Windows 3.x, Windows 95 uses DOS as its underlying operating system. DOS 7.0 is the version used by Windows 95; therefore DOS mode is simply a DOS 7.0 command prompt.

How can I enable multiboot?—In the Windows 95 environment, you can edit the MSDOS.SYS file to create a multiboot environment.

How do I install applications?—Most Windows applications include a Setup program that is designed to automatically install the application after you answer a few simple questions.

What are the symptoms of a stalled Windows 95 print spooler?—When the Windows 95 print spooler stalls, the operating system at first appears to hang (stop responding). After the operating system has recovered, you will notice that when you access the Printer folder, none of your printer icons appear. The fastest way to resolve a spooler problem in Windows 95 is to simply reboot the PC.

The printer won't print at all. Now what?—When working with a printer in any environment, you should always do the following:

- Verify that the printer, CMOS, and operating system are all configured to use the same type of cable (bidirectional, unidirectional, ECP, or EPP).

- Verify that the operating system has the correct printer driver installed.

- Check the spooler; be sure it has not stalled.

- Verify that the printer driver is configured to use the proper printer port (LPT1, COM1, or LPT2).

Where can I get more information about Windows 95?—You can purchase a Windows 95 user's manual, but it is easier and more cost-effective to use the built-in help features of Windows 95. To find Windows 95 Help, click the Start button and then click Help.

What is the Conflict troubleshooter?—The Conflict troubleshooter is an interactive help menu designed to resolve resource conflicts in the Windows 95 environment.

How do I get help?—All Microsoft operating systems are released with integrated Help. To quickly access the Help menu in Windows 95, press the F1 key.

What is REGEDIT and how do I execute it?—REGEDIT.EXE is a Windows-based utility that is used to manually modify the Windows registry. The REGEDIT utility can be found in the Windows directory and can be executed by double-clicking on it or by typing **REGEDIT** in the Run box. *Warning*: Using the REGEDIT utility can permanently damage an operating system.

A+ **CERTIFICATION OBJECTIVES**

Table 12-4   DOS/Windows A+ Objectives

Objectives	Chapters	Page Numbers
1.2 Identify ways to navigate the operating system and how to get to needed technical information.	1, 12	
B. Procedures for navigating through the Windows 3.x/Windows 95 operating system, accessing, and retrieving information.	1, 12	49, 50, 600, 601
3.3 Identify the basic system boot sequences, and alternative ways to boot the system software, including the steps to create an emergency boot disk with utilities installed.	2, 5, 7, 8, Appendix E	
D. Safe Mode	8, 12, Appendix E	425, 426 634, E5
E. DOS mode	8, 12, Appendix E	425, 426 635, E5
3.5 Identify the procedures for changing options, configuring, and using the Windows printing subsystem.	17	950, 951, 955
3.6 Identify the procedures for installing and launching typical Windows and non-Windows applications.	1	49, 50
4.1 Recognize and interpret the meaning of common error codes and startup messages from the boot sequence, and identify steps to correct the problems.	4, 5, 7, 8, 12, Appendices A and E	
A. Safe Mode	8, Appendix E	421, 428, E5
4.2 Recognize Windows-specific printing problems and identify the procedures for correcting them.	17	
A. Print spool is stalled	17	950
B. Incorrect/incompatible driver for print	17	951-955

12

Review Questions

Circle True or False.

1. You can configure your desktop wallpaper with the Control Panel Accessories option.
   True / False

2. In the Windows 95 environment, the desktop includes the wallpapered area of your screen.
   True / False

3. Shortcuts in Windows 95 are configured the same way as are shortcuts in Windows 3.x.
   True / False

4. The Start menu is a compilation of shortcuts. True / False

5. Describe how to create a new folder and add it to the Start menu.

   _____

   _____

   _____

   _____

   _____

6. Describe how to place a shortcut to My Computer in the Start menu.

_____

_____

_____

_____

_____

LAB 12.5 INSTALLING WINDOWS 98

Objective

The objective of this lab exercise is to install the Windows 98 operating system. After completing this lab exercise, you will be able to:

- Install Windows 98.
- Accurately describe the Windows 98 installation process.
- Locate and describe the function of Windows 98 system files.

Materials Required

This lab exercise requires one complete lab workstation for every four students. The lab workstations should meet the following requirements:

- 486DX\66 or better
- 24MB of RAM
- Windows 98 installation files
- 850MB hard drive

One DOS system disk

One blank formatted disk

A valid Windows 98 product ID for each lab workstation

Lab Setup & Safety Tips

- Each lab workstation should be preloaded with the Windows 98 installation files, which should be placed in a directory named C:\WIN98.

ACTIVITY

Installing Windows 98

1. Insert the system disk into drive A.

2. Power on your lab workstation and allow it to boot from the DOS system disk.

3. At the C prompt, type **CD C:\WIN98** and press **Enter**.

4. Type **SETUP** and press **Enter**.

5. Press **Enter** to allow the Setup program to run the SCANDISK utility.

6. Click the **Continue** button.

7. Click the option button next to the **I accept the agreement** statement.

8. Click the **Next** button.

9. Select the **Other Directory** option and click the **Next** button.

10. Type **C:\WINDOWS.98** and click the **Next** button.

11. Click the option button next to the **Typical** setup option, and then click the **Next** button.

12. Type your name and the name of the school you are attending.

13. Click the **Next** button.

14. Choose the **Recommended** Windows components by clicking the **Next** button.

12

15. Enter a computer name and workgroup name as indicated by your instructor.

16. Click the **Next** button.

17. Click the **Next** button to specify the United States as your country.

18. Click the **Next** button to begin creating an Emergency Startup Disk.

19. When prompted, insert a blank disk into the A drive and click the **OK** button.

20. Click the **OK** button when the operation has completed successfully.

21. Click the **Next** button, and the Setup program will begin copying the Windows 98 files to your hard drive.

22. Click the **OK** button and Setup will automatically restart your workstation.

23. You may be prompted to configure legacy devices that are attached to your workstation. (Note that the Setup program may need to be restarted before continuing to the next step.)

24. Click the list arrow to set the appropriate time zone and then click the **Close** button.

25. Click the **Cancel** button when prompted to configure a printer.

26. Click the **Restart Now** button.

Converting a FAT16 file system to FAT32

1. Click the **Start** button.

2. Point to **Programs** and then point to **Accessories**.

3. Point to **System Tools** and then click **Drive Converter(FAT32)**.

4. Click the **Next** button.

5. Select the drive that you want to convert by clicking it, and then click the **Next** button.

6. When you see a message that FAT32 will not be compatible with DOS or certain versions of Windows, click **OK**.

7. The Drive Converter wizard may prompt you to turn-off antivirus software or any other programs running in the background.

8. Click the **Next** button until you begin the conversion.

Lab Notes

What is the difference between Windows 95 and Windows 98?—There are very few differences between Windows 95 and Windows 98. The core of the operating systems is the same. However, Windows 98 added some utilities not available in Windows 95 and also has expanded on the compatibility of Windows 95. Many of the newer enchantments and utilities of Windows 98 are included in Table 12-5.

Table 12-5   Features in Windows 98 not available in Windows 95

Feature	Description
Troubleshooting utilities	Windows 95 has a few troubleshooting utilities, but the 15 utilities that come with Windows 98 are more interactive.
Update Wizard	The Update Wizard connects to the Microsoft Web site and automatically downloads any new drivers or fixes.
Maintenance Wizard	The Maintenance Wizard can be used to regularly schedule several maintenance tasks, including running Disk Defragmenter and ScanDisk, discussed in earlier chapters.
DriveSpace 3	An improved version of DriveSpace for Windows 95, it includes a third level of data compression called UltraPack, which takes up less space per file than does regular compression, called HiPack.
Power management support	Windows 98 supports some power management features, if both hardware and software are present to use them.
Registry Checker	Backs up and restores the registry.
Web tools and features	Several Windows 98 features take on an Internet look and feel. Windows 98 also supports viewing TV and interactive programs. You need a special TV interface card to use this feature.
FAT32	Recall that FAT32 is a file system that allows for a smaller cluster size on large drives than did the earlier FAT16.
New hardware support	With 1,200 device drivers, Windows 98 supports many more hardware devices than did Windows 95. Also, Windows 98 supports DMA channels for IDE CD-ROM drives, USB, DVD, and multiple video cards supporting multiple monitors.
Win32 Driver Model (WDM)	A new device driver model (also used by Windows NT), the Win 32 makes it possible for the same driver to be used by both operating systems.

12

A^+ | CERTIFICATION OBJECTIVES

Table 12-6   DOS/Windows A+ Objectives

Objectives	Chapters	Page Numbers
1.4 Identify the procedures for basic disk management.	5, 6, 7, Appendix F	
A. Using disk management utilities	6	320-322
E. Defragmenting	6	320-322
F. ScanDisk	6	322
G. FAT32	5, 6	248, 298-301
3.1 Identify the procedures for installing DOS, Windows 3.x, and Windows 95, and for bringing the software to a basic operational level.	6, 7, 12	
C. Run appropriate set up utility	7, 12	362, 637, 638
D. Loading drivers	12	611, 612
3.2 Identify steps to perform an operating system upgrade.	12	
A. Upgrading from DOS to Windows 95.	12	637, 638
3.3 Identify the basic system boot sequences, and alternative ways to boot the system software, including the steps to create an emergency boot disk with utilities installed.	2, 5, 7, 8, 12, Appendix E	
A. Files required to boot	2, 5	72, 261
B. Creating emergency boot disk	2, 5	103, 259-262
C. Startup disk	7	372, 373
D. Safe Mode	8, 12, Appendix E	425, 426, 634, E5

Review Questions

Circle True or False.

1. Windows 98 and Windows 95 have the same core operating system. True / False

2. FAT32 has a larger cluster size than FAT16. True / False

3. One of the features added to Windows 98 is USB compatibility. True / False

4. Windows 98 is compatible with drivers designed for Windows NT. True / False

5. List three utilities that are unique to Windows 98:

_____

_____

_____

_____

_____

6. Nancy has just completed installing her new USB hub and USB scanner. She also recently purchased a copy of Windows 98. Nancy currently is using the Windows 95 operating system. Describe the steps Nancy has to complete before she can use her USB scanner.

_____

_____

_____

_____

13

UNDERSTANDING AND SUPPORTING WINDOWS NT WORKSTATION

LAB 13.1 UPGRADING TO WINDOWS NT WORKSTATION

Objective

The objective of this lab exercise is to use the upgrade path from Windows 3.x to Windows NT 4.0. After completing this lab exercise, you will be able to:

- Upgrade from Window 3.x to Windows NT 4.0 Workstation.

- Describe the upgrade path from Windows 3.x to Windows NT 4.0.

Materials Required

This lab exercise requires one complete lab workstation for every four students. The lab workstations should meet the following requirements:

- 486 or better

- 16MB of RAM

- Installation files for Windows NT Workstation

A blank, formatted floppy disk

Lab Setup & Safety Tips

- Each lab workstation should have the Window 3.x operating system installed and functioning properly. Prior to the beginning of class, Windows NT installation files should be copied into a directory named C:\I386.

ACTIVITY

Upgrading to Windows NT Workstation

1. Power on your lab workstation and allow it to boot into Windows 3.x.

2. Open **Program Manager**.

3. Click the **File** menu.

4. Select **Run**.

5. Type **C:\I386\WINNT /B** and press **Enter**.

6. Press **Enter** when the copying is complete.

7. In the Program Manager, click **File** and select **Exit Windows**.

8. Click **OK** in the confirmation message box.

9. Power cycle your lab workstation.

10. Select the **NT Installation/Upgrade** option and press **Enter**.

11. Press the **Enter** key twice, until you see the license agreement.

12. Press the **Page Down** key several times through the license agreement.

13. Press the **F8** key to accept the license agreement.

14. Press **Enter** to accept the detected hardware defaults.

15. Press **Enter** three times until you restart your lab workstation.

16. Click the **Next** button to accept the defaults on the next few windows.

17. Type your name and press **Enter**.

18. Type the product ID provided by your instructor, and press **Enter**.

19. Type the lab workstation's name provided by your instructor, and press **Enter**.

20. Click the **Next** button to accept the defaults on the next four windows.

21. Click the **Select From List** option button.

22. Select the **Msloopback adapter** and click the **OK** button.

23. Click the **Next** button.

24. Clear the **TCP/IP** check box and click the **NetBeui** check box.

25. Click the **Next** button to accept the defaults on the next four windows.

26. Click the **Finish** button.

27. Select the proper time zone and click the **Close** button.

28. Click the **OK** button.

29. Click the **Test** button in the video display window and then click **OK**.

30. Click the **Yes** button.

31. Click the **OK** button to close the video display window.

32. Click the **OK** button.

33. Insert the blank, formatted floppy disk, and click the **OK** button.

34. Click the **Restart** button when prompted.

Lab Notes

Express Setup—Express Setup allows Windows NT to automatically install a group of preselected operating system components.

Custom Setup—Custom Setup allows you to select the components that you want to install.

13

Review Questions

Circle True or False.

1. Windows NT does not include an upgrade path from Windows 95. True / False

2. Windows NT is Plug-and-Play compliant. True / False

3. Windows NT includes Express, Custom, and Portable options similar to the Windows 95 Setup program. True / False

4. Windows NT is a 16-bit operating system. True / False

5. The difference between upgrading and installing Windows NT is that an upgrade always takes less time. True / False

6. Jim wants to install Windows NT on his PC. Jim has all of the necessary software, but doesn't have a NIC. Does Jim have to purchase a NIC before proceeding with the Windows NT installation? Explain your answer.

_____

_____

_____

_____

_____

LAB 13.2 INSTALLING WINDOWS NT WORKSTATION

Objective

The objective of this lab exercise is to install Windows NT Workstation. After completing this lab exercise, you will be able to:

- Install Windows NT Workstation.
- Create an emergency repair disk (ERD).

Materials Required

This lab exercise requires one complete lab workstation for every four students. The lab workstations should meet the following requirements:

- 486 or better
- 16MB of RAM
- CD-ROM drive

A set of Windows NT installation disks and an installation CD-ROM for each group of students

Lab Setup & Safety Tips

- The following activity will erase all data stored on drive C.

ACTIVITY

Installing Windows NT Workstation

1. Insert the Windows NT installation Disk 1 and allow your system to boot from drive A.
2. When prompted, insert Disk 2 and press **Enter**.
3. Press **Enter** on the next two windows.
4. Insert Disk 3 and press the **Enter** key.
5. Press the **Enter** key.
6. Press the **Page Down** button seven times.
7. Press the **F8** key.
8. Press the **Enter** key to accept the detected hardware defaults.
9. Select drive C and press the **Enter** key to install Windows NT.
10. Select the **Format the partition using the NTFS file system** option, and then press **Enter**.
11. Press the **F** key.
12. Press **Enter** to accept the default directory.
13. Press **Enter** to continue.
14. Remove the disk, and then press **Enter** to restart your computer.
15. Click the **Next** button to accept the defaults on the next two windows.
16. Type your name and click the **Next** button.
17. Enter the product ID and click the **Next** button.
18. Enter a computer name and click the **Next** button.
19. Enter a password and click the **Next** button.

20. Click the **Next** button to accept the defaults on the next three windows.

21. Select the **Do not connect this computer to a network at this time** option button.

22. Click the **Next** button.

23. Click the **Finish** button.

24. Select a time zone.

25. Click the **Close** button.

26. Click the **OK** button in the video display window.

27. Click the **Test** button in the video display window.

28. Click the **Yes** button to verify the display settings.

29. Click the **OK** button to close the video display window.

30. Click the **OK** button.

31. Insert a floppy disk, and then click the **OK** button.

32. Click the **Restart** button.

Lab Notes

What is NTFS all about?—NTFS stands for New Technology File System. Unlike FAT or VFAT, NTFS includes security built right into the file system. NTFS always maintains a cluster size of 4K, which greatly reduces space commonly wasted by large FAT volumes. (*Note*: Without special third-party software, an NTFS volume cannot be accessed from DOS.)

FAT vs. VFAT?—FAT stands for file allocation table and is the file system that was introduced with MS-DOS. Since then Microsoft has updated FAT to be used in the Windows 95 environment; this update is VFAT. The V stands for Virtual. VFAT is an additional area in FAT that is reserved to store long filename information. Note that VFAT and FAT32 are not the same type of file system.

What is an ERD?—ERD stands for emergency repair disk. An ERD contains a backup copy of your Windows NT registry. Each ERD is designed specifically for the operating system that created it; ERDs are not interchangeable.

How do you make an ERD?—An ERD can be created during the Windows NT installation or at any time after Windows NT has been installed. To create an ERD after Windows NT has been installed, click the Start button, point to Programs, and click Command Prompt. Type RDISK /S. The RDISK utility is used to create an ERD and the /S tells Windows NT not only to back up the registry files, but also to include the Windows NT security file (SAM).

13

CERTIFICATION OBJECTIVES

Table 13-1   DOS/Windows A+ Objectives

Objectives	Chapters	Page Numbers
1.4 Identify the procedures for basic disk management.		
G. FAT32	5, 6	248, 298-301
I. Virtual file allocation tables (VFAT)	6	300-301

Review Questions

Circle True or False.

1. To install Windows NT you must have a network interface card. True / False

2. The Windows NT installation gives you the option to create and delete partitions. True / False

3. Windows NT allows you to configure a network interface card during the installation process. True / False

4. The Windows NT operating system does not support PCs that use a 486 processor. True / False

5. What is the name of the directory that contains the Windows NT installation files for x86 computers?

_____

6. List the four questions you have to answer during the installation of Windows NT.

_____

_____

_____

_____

_____

LAB 13.3 CUSTOMIZING AND REPAIRING WINDOWS NT WORKSTATION

Objective

This lab exercise is designed to provide you the opportunity to configure some common settings in the Windows NT environment. After completing this lab exercise, you will be able to:

- Configure Windows NT to use customized shortcuts.
- Use an ERD to repair a Windows NT installation.
- View and modify the Boot.ini file.
- Install a printer driver in the Windows NT environment.

Materials Required

This lab exercise requires one complete lab workstation for every four students. The lab workstations should meet the following requirements:

- 486 or better
- 16MB of RAM
- CD-ROM drive

The Windows NT workstation disks and CD-ROM

An ERD for each lab workstation

Lab Setup & Safety Tips

- Each lab workstation should have Windows NT installed and functioning properly.

13

ACTIVITY

Using shortcuts to manage memory

1. Right-click the desktop, and then point to **New** on the shortcut menu.
2. Click **Shortcut**.
3. Type **C:\WINNT\SYSTEM32\WINFILE.EXE** and press **Enter**.
4. In the Select a name for the shortcut box, type **File Manager**.
5. Click the **Finish** button.
6. Right-click the newly created **File Manager** shortcut.
7. Select **Properties** from the shortcut menu to see the Properties dialog box illustrated in Figure 13-1.
8. Click the **Shortcut** tab.
9. Observe the location of the **Run in Separate Memory Space** check box.

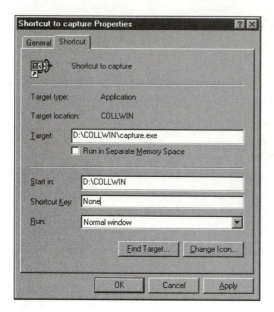

Figure 13-1 Properties dialog box for a 16-bit Windows

Using your textbook for reference, answer the following questions:

1. How does Windows NT respond when the Run in Separate Memory Space check box is checked?

_____

_____

_____

_____

_____

2. What does it mean when the Run in Separate Memory Space check box is dimmed?

_____

_____

_____

_____

_____

Repairing a Windows NT installation

1. Insert the Windows NT installation Disk 1 and allow your system to boot from drive A.

2. Insert Disk 2 and press **Enter**.

3. Press **Enter**.

4. Press the letter **R** key.

5. Press **Enter** on the next two windows.

6. Insert Disk 3 and press **Enter**.

7. Press the **Enter** key on the next three windows.

8. Insert the emergency repair disk.

9. Insert the Windows NT CD-ROM. If necessary, type **A** to repair all files.

10. Press **Enter** to restart the computer.

Installing a printer driver

1. Power on your lab workstation and allow it to boot into Windows NT.

2. Double-click the **My Computer** icon.

3. Double-click the **Printers** folder

4. Double-click **Add Printer**.

5. Click the **Next** button.

6. Click the **My computer** option and click the **Next** button.

7. Select the appropriate printer port and click the **Next** button.

8. Choose the correct printer driver by first selecting the appropriate manufacturer, and then selecting the printer model. Click the **Next** button when you are done.

9. Click the **Next** button again to use the default printer name.

10. If necessary, click the **Next** button to accept the default on the next window.

11. Click the **Finish** button to complete the driver installation.

Lab Notes
Repairing Windows NT—Windows NT includes a repair process as part of its Setup program. If a Windows NT installation becomes damaged or corrupt, you can use the Setup program to repair it.

Review Questions

Circle True or False.

1. The Windows NT repair process can be used to reinstall Windows if it becomes damaged. True / False

2. An ERD is always necessary when using the emergency repair process. True / False

3. A CD-ROM drive must be present to execute the emergency repair process. True / False

4. The Run in Separate Memory Space check box tells Windows NT to store that application in the swap file at all times. True / False

5. List two tasks that the Windows NT repair process can be used to accomplish.

_____

_____

_____

_____

6. Janet's Windows NT workstation has been rendered useless by a virus. You are Janet's PC support technician and have cleaned the virus but the system still won't boot properly. Janet does not have an ERD. Describe how you would attempt to restore Janet's PC without reinstalling Windows NT.

_____

_____

_____

_____

13

LAB 13.4 THE WINDOWS NT REGISTRY

Objective

The objective of this lab exercise is to enable you to understand and modify the Windows NT registry. After completing this lab exercise, you will be able to:

- Name and describe some different values commonly used in the registry.
- Create and modify registry values.

Materials Required

This lab exercise requires one complete lab workstation for every four students. The lab workstation should meet the following requirements:

- 486 or better
- 16MB of RAM
- Windows NT Workstation

Lab Setup & Safety Tips

- Each lab workstation should have Windows NT installed and functioning properly.

ACTIVITY

Viewing the registry

1. Allow your lab workstation to boot into Windows NT.
2. Log on to Windows NT.
3. Click the **Start** button.
4. Select **Run**.
5. Type **REGEDIT** and press **Enter**.
6. Using the registry editor, locate an example of a key, hive, and each type of value, listed below. Write the path to each example on the lines provided.

   Hive

   _____

   _____

   Key

   _____

   _____

   Binary value

   _____

   _____

   String value

   _____

   _____

DWord value

_____

_____

Modifying the right-click menu using the Registry Editor

1. Click the **Start** button.

2. Select **Run**.

3. Type **REGEDIT** and press **Enter**.

4. Double-click the **HKEY_LOCAL_MACHINE** hive.

5. Double-click the **Software** key.

6. Double-click the **Classes** key.

7. Double-click the **Directory** key.

8. Double-click the **Shell** key.

9. Click the **Edit** menu and point to **New**.

10. Click **Key**.

11. Type **File Manager** and press **Enter**.

12. Double-click the **File Manager** key, if necessary.

13. Click the **Edit** menu and point to **New**.

14. Click **Key**.

15. Type **Command** and press **Enter**.

16. Look at the right window in the Registry Editor, and locate the value **Default** (this is a string value).

17. Right-click the **Default** string value and select **Modify** from the menu.

18. Type **C:\WINNT\SYSTEM32\WINFILE.EXE**.

19. Click the **OK** button.

20. Click the **Close** button to close the Registry Editor.

Testing your work

1. Right-click the **Start** button.

   There should now be a File Manager option on this menu.

2. Click the **File Manager** option.

   If your registry entries are completed correctly, File Manager will launch.

Lab Notes
Where is the Windows NT registry stored?—The Windows NT registry is stored in two centralized locations: C:\%systemroot%\system32\config. The user registry is stored in the user's personal profile.

What is the difference between REGEDIT and REGEDT32?—The REGEDIT utility has the ability to perform complex registry searches but cannot modify permissions of registry keys. REGEDT32 has the ability to modify permissions, but cannot conduct any type of registry search functions.

Review Questions

Circle True or False.

1. Using the Registry Editor is an excellent way for beginning PC users to learn more about the operating system on their computer. True / False

2. REGEDIT can modify permissions. True / False

3. Windows NT stores its registry in one file named REG.DAT. True / False

4. One example of a key is HKEY_LOCAL_MACHINE. True / False

5. Windows NT stores each user's personal registry information in the user's profile directory. True / False

6. Jamie wants to use the Registry Editor to change her Netscape proxy configuration, but she is not familiar with the Registry Editor utility. In the space below describe how Jamie can use the REGEDIT utility to search for her current proxy settings.

_____

_____

_____

_____

_____

PURCHASING A PC OR BUILDING YOUR OWN

LABS INCLUDED IN THIS CHAPTER

LAB 14.1   BUILDING A NEW PC: PART 1

LAB 14.2   BUILDING A NEW PC: PART 2

LAB 14.3   BUILDING A NEW PC: PART 3

LAB 14.1 BUILDING A NEW PC: PART 1

Objective

The objective of this lab exercise is to begin building a PC. This lab exercise combines the skills you have learned in previous exercises and allows you more hands-on practice to further develop your hardware skills. After completing this lab exercise, you will be able to:

- Install a systemboard.
- Install a CPU.
- Install RAM.

Materials Required

For this lab exercise, students need tools to complete the installation of the following components:

One PC case

One Pentium systemboard

Two 8MB SIMMS

One Pentium CPU

One CPU cooling fan

Thermal grease

Lab Setup & Safety Tips

- Students must comply with standard ESD procedures.
- Students should have documentation that states the correct systemboard jumper and DIP switch settings for the CPU they are using for this activity.
- Before beginning this activity, students should verify and, if necessary, reconfigure the systemboard to use the proper jumper and DIP switch settings.

ACTIVITY

Installing the CPU

1. Place the systemboard on the ESD mat.
2. Remove the CPU from its package, and note the blunt end on the processor.
3. Locate the ZIF on the systemboard and unlatch the lever.
4. Install the CPU by first matching the blunt end of the ZIF with the blunt end of the CPU and then gently pressing down on the CPU.
5. Don't force the CPU. If it is not moving into place with ease, check for bent pins on the bottom of the CPU. Also verify that you have it lined up properly with the ZIF.
6. Lock the CPU into position using the ZIF lever.
7. Coat the bottom of the CPU fan with thermal grease.
8. Place the CPU fan on top of the CPU.
9. Lock the CPU fan into position.

Installing the RAM

1. Locate the SIMM banks on your systemboard.

2. Place the first SIMM at a 45° angle and gently slide it into bank zero.

3. Slowly push the SIMM upright until it snaps into position.

4. Repeat steps 1, 2, and 3 for bank 1.

Mounting the systemboard

The process of mounting a systemboard varies from PC to PC because of the different case designs available. The following Lab Notes discuss some of the similarities between cases.

1. Locate the screws and standoffs necessary for mounting your systemboard.

2. Line up the systemboard with the case to determine where the screws and standoffs will be placed.

   Note: Any screws used must be placed within an area on the systemboard that allows for metal to metal contact. If you are unsure, consult the systemboard user's manual.

3. Install the standoffs.

4. Mount the systemboard and lock the standoffs into place, if necessary.

5. Secure all screws.

6. Locate the P8 and P9 power connectors.

7. Attach the P8 and P9 power connectors. Be sure the black wires of each connector are placed side-by-side.

Lab Notes

What voltage is my CPU?—Different types of CPUs use different voltage settings. Consult your CPU support documentation for details. *Note:* Some CPUs have the voltage marked on the CPU.

What divisor should I use?—The divisor varies from system to system. Consult your support documentation for the systemboard and the CPU for more details.

Where is pin one found on a CPU?—You can find pin one on a CPU by locating the flat edge of the processor and aligning it with the flat edge of the ZIF on the systemboard. When you look at a processor, three of the four edges will be squared, but the fourth will appear flat. The flat corner is pin one.

14

A^+ CERTIFICATION OBJECTIVES

Table 14-1 Core A+ Objectives

Objectives	Chapters	Page Numbers
1.2 Identify basic procedures for adding and removing field replaceable modules.	1, 3, 4, 11, 14	
A. System board	1	14
B. Storage device	1, 14	11, 774-779
C. Power supply	1, 11, 14	19, 575, 576, 766-771
D. Processor /CPU	3, 14	115, 760-763
E. Memory	1, 4, 14	11, 228-229, 763, 764, 766

Review Questions

Circle True or False.

1. Systemboards are designed to use specific types of CPUs.   True / False

2. You must align pin one when installing a CPU.   True / False

3. Use standoffs to keep the systemboard from touching the case and shorting the entire PC. True / False

4. All systemboards require a minimum of 8 screws.   True / False

5. The P8 and P9 power connectors supply power to the systemboard.   True / False

6. One of your coworkers, Joe, is installing a CPU. After several attempts, Joe decides to call you for help. Describe to Joe how to identify in which direction the CPU should be installed.

   _____
   _____
   _____
   _____
   _____

7. Which banks must always be included when installing RAM and why?

   _____
   _____
   _____
   _____
   _____

LAB 14.2 BUILDING A NEW PC: PART 2

Objective

The objective of this lab exercise is to continue building the PC you began in Lab 14.1. This lab exercise allows you to further develop your hardware installation and configuration skills. After completing this lab exercise you will be able to:

- Install COM and LPT ports.
- Install a hard drive.
- Install a CD-ROM drive.
- Install a floppy drive.

Materials Required

The partial lab workstation from the exercise in Lab 14.1

One Cable Select data cable

One hard drive

One CD-ROM drive

The COM and LPT ports included with the systemboard

One floppy drive

The tools necessary to complete the installation of the components listed above

Lab Setup & Safety Tips

- Students should have documentation describing the jumper settings for the hard drive and CD-ROM drive prior to starting the activity.
- Students must comply with standard ESD procedures.

14

ACTIVITY

Installing the COM and LPT ports

1. Locate the COM and LPT ports packaged with the systemboard.
2. Locate two available expansion slots within the case (you will not need any available expansion slots on the systemboard).
3. Remove any blanks that might be in place.
4. Locate the pins for the LPT cable.
5. Attach the LPT cable to the systemboard. Be sure that pin one is aligned with the red stripe on the data cable.
6. Slide the LPT port into place and secure it with a screw.
7. Locate the pins for the COM ports.
8. Attach the COM port cables to the systemboard. Be sure that the pins are aligned correctly.
9. Slide the COM ports into place and secure them with a screw.

Installing the hard drive

1. Locate an available bay for the hard drive.

2. Remove any blanks that might be in place.

3. Slide the hard drive into the bay.

4. Jumper the hard drive to the cable select position.

5. Connect the IDE data cable to the systemboard. Be sure to verify that the red line on the data cable matches the pin 1 marking on the systemboard.

6. Connect the IDE data cable and the power connector. Note that the hard drive should be attached to the IDE connector closest to the systemboard.

7. Mount the hard drive.

Installing the CD-ROM drive

1. Locate an available bay for the CD-ROM drive.

2. Remove any blanks that might be in place.

3. Slide the CD-ROM drive into the bay.

4. Jumper the CD-ROM drive to the cable select position.

5. Connect the IDE data cable and the power connector. Note that the CD-ROM drive should be attached to the IDE connector farthest from the systemboard. Also connect the audio cable to the sound card.

6. Mount the CD-ROM drive.

Installing the floppy drive

1. Locate an available 3.5-inch drive bay.

2. Remove any blanks that might be in place.

3. Slide the 3.5-inch floppy drive into the bay.

4. Plug in the data cable.

5. Plug in the power connector.

Lab Notes

I/O ports—This lab exercise assumes that both the COM and LPT ports were included with the systemboard at the time of purchase. Note that this is not always the case and, at times, you may need to purchase a separate I/O card.

A^+ | **CERTIFICATION OBJECTIVES**

Table 14-2   Core A+ Objectives

Objectives	Chapters	Page Numbers
1.2 Identify basic procedures for adding and removing field replaceable modules.	1, 3, 4, 11, 14	
B. Storage device	1, 14	11, 774-779
F. Input devices	1, 14	5, 14, 780-782
1.5 Identify proper procedures for installing and configuring IDE/EIDE devices.	6, 7	
A. Master/Slave	6, 7	282, 348-354
B. Devices per channel	6, 7	282, 348-354
1.7 Identify proper procedures for installing and configuring peripheral devices.	14, 15	
C. Storage devices	14	781, 782

Review Questions

Circle **True** or **False**.

1. COM ports don't follow the pin one rule.   **True** or **False**

2. Cable Select is the same as master and slave.   **True** or **False**

3. CD-ROMs must always be slave.   **True** or **False**

4. A CD-ROM should not be mounted next to a hard drive because it has a magnetic field that could erase data from the hard drive.   **True** or **False**

5. List three ways an IDE CD-ROM could be jumpered to function properly with only one other hard drive present.

_____

_____

_____

_____

6. How are the COM ports affected when a systemboard's LPT port is an embedded component?

_____

_____

_____

_____

14

LAB 14.3 BUILDING A NEW PC: PART 3

Objective

The objective of this lab exercise is to finish building the PC that you began in Labs 14.1 and 14.2. This lab exercise allows you to further develop your hardware installation and configuration skills. After completing this lab exercise, you will be able to:

- Install a video card.

- Install a sound card.

- Install a network card.

- Describe how resources are allocated throughout your PC.

- Complete the final PC configuration steps and describe the value of allowing a system burn-in period.

Materials Required

The partial lab workstation from the exercise in Lab 14.2

One PCI video card

One 16-bit ISA sound card

One network interface card

The tools necessary to complete the installation of the components listed above

Lab Setup & Safety Tips

- Students must comply with standard ESD procedures.

- Students should receive documentation describing the jumper settings for the sound card and the network interface card prior to starting the activity.

ACTIVITY

Installing the video card

1. Locate the PCI video card.

2. Locate one available PCI expansion slot.

3. Remove any blanks that may be in place.

4. Gently slide the video card into the PCI slot. Be careful not to bend the video card from side to side.

5. Secure the video card with a screw.

Installing the sound card

1. Locate the sound card.

2. Write down your sound card's jumper configuration and verify that it does not conflict with any other devices.

_____

_____

_____

3. Locate one available ISA expansion slot.

4. Remove any blanks that might be in place.

5. Gently slide the sound card into the ISA slot. Be careful not to bend the sound card from side to side.

6. Secure the sound card with a screw, and connect the audio cable to the sound card and the back of the CD–ROM drive, if necessary.

Installing the network interface card

1. Locate the network interface card.

2. Write down your network card's jumper configuration, and verify that it does not conflict with any other devices.

   _____

   _____

   _____

3. Locate one available ISA expansion slot.

4. Remove any blanks that may be in place.

5. Gently slide the network card into the ISA slot. Be careful not to bend the network card from side to side.

6. Secure the network card with a screw.

Completing your resources worksheet

On the lines below, record the resources used by each device.

COM1 _____

COM2 _____

LPT1 _____

LPT2 _____

Sound card   _____

   _____

Network card _____

   _____

Completing the final steps

1. Thoroughly inspect the case. Look for loose wires and any metal (screws, blanks, etc.) that could cause a short.

2. Replace the top to the case.

3. Plug in the monitor.

4. Plug in the keyboard.

5. Plug in the mouse.

6. Secure the LAN line (if available).

7. Connect speakers (if available).

8. Connect all power cords.

9. Power on the PC for the first time.

14

10. Enter the CMOS Setup program.

11. Set the date and time.

12. Set the correct configuration for each of the hardware components.

13. Save your changes and reboot.

14. Install an operating system.

15. Allow at least 24 hours for a system burn-in period.

Lab Notes

How do I modify the resources of an integrated network card?—When network cards are integrated, you can modify their resources by using the CMOS Setup program.

What is system burn-in?—System burn-in refers to the testing of new hardware. After a PC has been assembled and each component has been tested for functionality, most technicians allow the system at least 24 hours to burn in. During the system burn-in period, the computer is left powered on with an operating system installed and configured properly. Because new hardware components often show any faults during the first 24 to 48 hours of use, the system burn-in period detects these faults before the computer is released to a customer.

A⁺ CERTIFICATION OBJECTIVES

Table 14-3 Core A+ Objectives

Objectives	Chapters	Page Numbers
1.3 Identify available IRQs, DMAs, and I/O addresses and procedures for configuring them for device installation.	2, 5, 7, 9	
A. Standard IRQ settings	2, 9	83, 90, 463
1.7 Identify proper procedures for installing and configuring peripheral devices.	14, 15	
A. Monitor/Video Card	14	765, 766
1.8 Identify concepts and procedures relating to BIOS.	2, 3	
A. Methods for upgrading	2, 3	89, 138-140
B. When to upgrade	2, 3	135-136, 138-140
7.1 Identify basic networking concepts, including how a network works.	15, 16	
C. Network Interface Cards	16	869-872
F. Ways to network a PC	16	861-864, 877, 878, 883, 884

Review Questions

Circle True or False.

1. You must always install the video card before the sound card.   True or False

2. Most sound cards use IRQ 9 by default.   True or False

3. All network interface cards require DMA 3.   True or False

4. PCI video cards are faster than ISA video cards.   True or False

5. Before powering on a system, you should always look for loose wires or pieces of metal. True or False

6. Name three CMOS settings that must be modified after a PC is powered on for the first time.

_____

_____

_____

_____

_____

7. Describe how a system burn-in period affects a product's quality.

_____

_____

_____

_____

_____

14

COMMUNICATING OVER PHONE LINES

LAB 15.1 COMMUNICATIONS AND DOS/WINDOWS 3.x

Objective

The objective of this lab exercise is to install and configure an AT-compatible modem. After completing this lab exercise, you will be able to:

- Install an internal modem.
- Use AT commands to control a modem.
- Use the Windows 3.x Terminal program.

Materials Required

This lab exercise requires one complete lab workstation for every four students. The lab workstations should meet the following requirements:

- 486 or better
- 4MB of RAM
- Windows 3.x

One internal modem

One analog phone line for each lab workstation

One ESD mat

Grounding straps for each student

Tools necessary to remove the case and install an internal modem

Lab Setup & Safety Tips

- Students must comply with standard ESD procedures.
- Students should have documentation describing the jumper settings for the internal modem prior to beginning the activities.

ACTIVITY

Installing a modem

1. Power off and unplug your lab workstation.
2. Remove the case.
3. Locate an available ISA slot for the internal modem.
4. Remove any blanks that might be in place.
5. Configure the modem's jumpers to use an available COM port.
6. Gently install the modem into the ISA slot. *Warning*: Be careful not to bend the modem from side to side.
7. Secure the modem with a screw.
8. Plug in the lab workstation.
9. Stand clear of the lab workstation and power it on.
10. Enter the CMOS Setup program.
11. Verify that the modem is not conflicting with an existing COM port.
12. If the modem is conflicting with a COM port, disable the COM port.

13. Save your changes and reboot the PC.

14. Power off your lab workstation.

15. Unplug the power cord.

16. Replace the case.

17. Plug in the power cord.

18. Stand clear of your lab workstation, power it on, and allow it to boot into Windows 3.x.

Dialing with Terminal

1. Double-click the **Accessories** group icon.

2. Double-click the **Terminal** icon. (If you have not run Terminal on this PC before, a window will open; click the **Cancel** button to close the window.)

3. Click the **Settings** menu.

4. Click the **Communications** option.

5. Configure the Terminal program to use the following settings:

   Baud rate: **19200**
   Data bits: **8**
   Parity: **None**
   Flow Control: **Xon/Xoff**
   Stop bits: **1**
   Connector: (choose the COM port of the installed modem)

6. Click the **OK** button.

7. Click the **Phone** menu.

8. Select **Dial**.

9. Type the phone number you want to dial.

10. Click the **OK** button.

11. To end a call, click the **Phone** menu.

12. Click **Hangup**.

Using AT commands

1. Double-click the **Accessories** group icon.

2. Double-click the **Terminal** icon.

3. Click the **Settings** menu.

4. Click the **Communications** option.

5. Configure the Terminal program to use the following settings:

   Baud rate: **19200**
   Data bits: **8**
   Parity: **None**
   Flow Control: **Xon/Xoff**
   Stop bits: **1**
   Connector: (choose the COM port of the installed modem)

6. Click the **OK** button.

7. In the Terminal window, type **ATZ** and press **Enter** to reset the modem.

15

8. Type **ATDT ########** where **########** represents a phone number you want to dial.

9. Press **Enter**.

10. Type **ATH** and press **Enter** to hang up the phone.

11. Type **ATZ** and press **Enter**.

Table 15-1   Some examples of AT commands

Command	Description
ATDT 5552115	Dial the given number using tone dialing.
ATDP 5552115	Dial the given number using pulse dialing.
ATD 9,5552115	Dial 9 and pause, then dial the remaining numbers (use this method to get an outside line from a business phone).
AT &F1DT9,5552115	Restore the default factory settings. Dial using tone dialing. Pause after dialing the 9. Dial the remaining numbers.
ATM2L2	Always have the speaker on. Set loudness of the speaker at medium.
ATI3	Report the modem ROM version.

Table 15-2   AT commands for Hayes-compatible modems

Command	Description	Some Values and Their Meanings
+++	**Escape sequence:** Tells the modem to return to command mode. You should pause at least 1 second before you begin the sequence. After you end it, wait another second before you send another command. Don't begin this command with AT.	
On	**Go online:** Tells the modem to return to online data mode. This is the reverse command from the escape sequence above.	O0 Return online O1 Return online and retrain (perform training or handshaking again with the remote modem)
A/	**Repeat last command:** Repeat the last command performed by the modem. Don't begin the command with AT, but do follow it with Enter. Useful when redialing a busy number.	
In	**Identification:** Instructs the modem to return product identification information.	I0 Return the product code I3 Return the modem ROM version
Zn	**Reset:** Instructs the modem to reset and restore the configuration to that defined at power on.	Z0 Reset and return to user profile 0 Z1 Reset and return to user profile 1
&F	**Factory default:** Instructs the modem to reload the factory default profile. In most cases, use this command to reset the modem rather than the Z command.	
A	**Answer the phone:** Instructs the modem to answer the phone, transmit the answer tone, and wait for a carrier from the remote modem.	

Table 15-2   AT commands for Hayes-compatible modems (continued)

Command	Description	Some Values and Their Meanings
Dn	**Dial:** Tells the modem to dial a number. There are several parameters that can be added to this command. A few are listed on the right.	D5551212 Dial the given number D, Causes the dialing to pause DP Use pulse dialing DT Use tone dialing DW Wait for dial tone D& Wait for the credit card dialing tone before continuing with the remaining dial string
Hn	**Hang up:** Tells the modem to hang up.	H0 Hang up H1 Hang up and enter command mode
Mn	**Speaker control:** Instructs the modem in how it is to use its speaker.	M0 Speaker always off M1 Speaker on until carrier detect M2 Speaker always on
Ln	**Loudness:** Sets the loudness of the modem's speaker.	L1 Low L2 Medium L3 High
Xn	**Response:** Tells the modem how it is to respond to a dial tone and busy signal.	X0 Blind dialing; the modem does not need to hear the dial tone first and will not hear a busy signal X4 Modem must first hear the dial tone and responds to a busy signal (this is the default value)

Lab Notes

What are AT commands?—AT commands are a set of standardized modem commands that all Hayes-compatible modems can understand.

15

CERTIFICATION OBJECTIVES

Table 15-3   Core A+ Objectives

Objectives	Chapters	Page Numbers
1.1 Identify basic terms, concepts, and functions of system modules, including how each module should work during normal operation.	1, 2, 11, 15	
E. Modem	1, 15	18, 803, 804
F. Firmware	1	21, 25
H. BIOS	1	21, 25
I. CMOS	1	8
1.3 Identify available IRQs, DMAs, and I/O addresses and procedures for configuring them for device installation.	2, 5, 7, 9	
A. Standard IRQ settings	2, 9	83, 90, 463
B. Modems	9	455, 456
1.7 Identify proper procedures for installing and configuring peripheral devices.	14, 15	
B. Modem	14, 15	781, 782, 825-828

A+   CERTIFICATION OBJECTIVES

Table 15-4   DOS/Windows A+ Objectives

Objective	Chapters	Page Numbers
5.2 Identify concepts and capabilities relating to the Internet and basic procedures for setting up a system for Internet access.	16, 18	
H. Dial-up access	16	879-882, 912-915

Review Questions

Circle True or False.

1. A modem could never conflict with a COM port. True / False

2. You can use the Terminal program to test a modem. True / False

3. ATDT and ATZ are examples of AT commands. True / False

4. You use the ATDT command to reset an AT-compatible modem. True / False

5. How should an AT-compatible modem respond to the ATH command?

_____

_____

_____

_____

_____

6. Write the AT commands necessary to reset, dial, and hang up an AT-compatible modem.

_____

_____

_____

_____

_____

LAB 15.2 COMMUNICATIONS AND WINDOWS 9x

Objective

The objective of this lab exercise is to enable you to install and configure all the necessary components to create a functional Dial-Up Networking connection in Windows 9x. After completing this lab exercise, you will be able to:

- Install Dial-Up Networking.

- Install a modem device driver.

- Install the dial-up adapter.

- Configure Windows 9x to use a PPP dial-up connection.

Materials Required

This lab exercise requires one complete lab workstation for every four students. The lab workstations should meet the following requirements:

- 486 or better

- 8MB of RAM

- Windows 9x

One internal modem

Lab Setup & Safety Tips

- Each lab workstation should have Windows 9x installed and functioning properly.

ACTIVITY

Installing Dial-Up Networking

1. Power on your lab workstation and allow it to boot into Windows 9x.

2. Click the **Start** button.

3. Point to **Settings**.

4. Click **Control Panel**.

5. Double-click the **Add/Remove Programs** icon.

6. Click the **Windows Setup** tab.

7. In the list of components, double-click **Communications**.

8. Click the **Dial-Up Networking** check box to select it.

9. Click the **OK** button to close the Communications dialog box.

10. Click the **OK** button.

11. If prompted, enter the path to the installation files.

15

Installing a modem driver

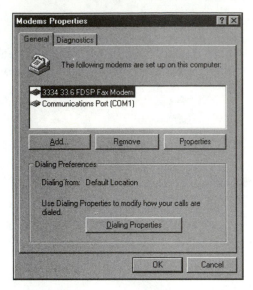

Figure 15-1 Maximum modem speed is often part of the modem name (in this case 33.6 Kbps)

1. Click the **Start** button.

2. Point to **Settings**.

3. Click **Control Panel**.

4. Double-click the **Modems** icon.

5. If you are not prompted to install a modem, click the **Add** button.

6. Click the **Next** button to have Windows 9x search for a modem.

7. Verify that Windows 9x has detected the correct type of modem. You may have to provide a disk if Windows cannot detect your modem.

8. Click the **Next** button.

9. Click the **Finish** button.

10. Click the **OK** button.

Installing the dial-up adapter

This exercise assumes that you do not have any networking components installed. Prior to beginning this activity, remove any networking components that might be present.

1. Click the **Start** button.

2. Point to **Settings**.

3. Click **Control Panel**.

4. Double-click the **Network** icon.

5. Click the **Add** button.

6. In the type of component list, double-click **Client**.

7. Select **Microsoft** from the Manufacturer list.

8. Double-click the **Client for Microsoft Networks** option.

9. Click **Add** and then double-click **Adapter** in the Type of component list.

10. Select **Microsoft** from the Manufacturer list.

11. In the list of installed network components, double-click the **Dial-Up Adapter** option.

12. Click the **Add** button.

13. In the list of network components, double-click the **Protocol** option.

14. Select **Microsoft** from the Manufacturer list.

15. Double-click the **TCP/IP** option.

16. Click the **OK** button.

17. If prompted, enter the path to the installation files.

18. Click the **Yes** button when prompted to restart your computer.

Creating and configuring a dialer

1. Double-click the **My Computer** icon.

2. Double-click the **Dial-Up Networking** icon.

3. Double-click **Make New Connection**.

4. Type **Lab Dialer** in the Type a name for the computer you are dialing text box, and click the **Next** button.

5. Type **555-5555** in the Telephone Number box.

6. Click the **Next** button.

7. Click the **Finish** button.

8. In the Dial-up Networking window, right-click the **Lab Dialer** icon.

9. Select **Properties** from the menu.

10. Click the **Server Types** button.

11. Verify that the type of dial-up server is set to the **PPP Windows 95**, **Windows NT 3.5, Internet** option or the **PPP: Internet, Windows NT Server, Windows 98 option**.

12. Clear the NetBeui and the IPX/SPX check boxes in the **Allowed Network Protocols** list.

13. Click the **TCP/IP** Settings button.

14. Click the **Specify Name Server Addresses** option button.

15. Type the primary DNS address, provided by your instructor, in the primary DNS box.

16. Click the **OK** button to close the TCP/IP Settings dialog box.

17. Click the **OK** button to close the Server Types dialog box.

18. Click **OK** to close the Lab Dialer dialog box.

15

 Lab Notes

What is the difference between the modem driver and the dial-up adapter?—You install a modem driver using the Modems option in the Control Panel. The modem driver ensures proper communication between the operating system and the modem's hardware. The dial-up adapter is a dial-up networking component that is not necessary to use the modem but is necessary to connect using some protocols such as PPP.

What is a dialer?—A dialer is a Windows 9x object that contains settings for a particular dial-up connection, such as phone numbers, IP addresses, and allowed protocols. In Windows 9x you can create and configure multiple dialers, each of which can contain a different configuration.

CERTIFICATION OBJECTIVES

Table 15-5   DOS/Windows A+ Objectives

Objective	Chapters	Page Numbers
5.2 Identify concepts and capabilities relating to the Internet and basic procedures for setting up a system for Internet access.	16, 18	
H. Dial-up access	16	879-882, 912-915

Review Questions

Circle True or False.

1. Dial-Up Networking is installed by using the Add New Hardware option found in the Control Panel. True / False

2. Modem drivers are installed using the Modems option in the Control Panel. True / False

3. All dialers must be configured to dial the same phone number. True / False

4. Dialers are created using the Make New Connection option in the Dial-Up Networking folder. True / False

5. Joy has just purchased and installed a new modem. She has Windows 9x installed on her PC. What should Joy do next so her operating system will properly communicate with her modem?

    _____

    _____

    _____

    _____

    _____

6. List four configurable options in a Windows 9x dialer.

    _____

    _____

    _____

    _____

    _____

LAB 15.3 COMMUNICATIONS AND WINDOWS NT

Objective

The objective of this lab exercise is to enable you to install and configure all the necessary components to create a functional Dial-Up Networking connection using the Remote Access Service. After completing this lab exercise you will be able to:

- Install a modem device driver.
- Install the remote access service (RAS).
- Configure Windows NT to use a PPP dial-up connection.

Materials Required

This lab exercise requires one complete lab workstation for every four students. The lab workstations should meet the following requirements:

- 486 or better
- 16MB of RAM
- Windows NT
- One internal modem

Lab Setup & Safety Tips

- Each lab workstation should have Windows NT installed and functioning properly.

ACTIVITY

Installing a modem driver

1. Power on your lab workstation and allow it to boot into Windows NT.
2. Log on to your Windows NT system as **Administrator** or an equivalent account.
3. Click the **Start** button.
4. Point to **Settings**.
5. Click **Control Panel**.
6. Double-click the **Modems** icon.
7. If you are not prompted to install a modem, click the **Add** button.
8. Click the **Next** button to have Windows NT search for a modem.
9. Verify that Windows NT has detected the correct type of modem. You may have to provide a disk if Windows cannot detect your modem.
10. Click the **Next** button.
11. Click the **Finish** button.
12. Click the **Close** button.

15

Installing the RAS

Figure 15-2 Dial-Up Networking installation

1. Double-click the **My Computer** icon.

2. Double-click the **Dial-Up Networking** icon. You see the Dial-Up Networking dialog box, illustrated in Figure 15-2.

2. When prompted, click the **Install** button.

3. If prompted, insert the Windows NT CD and enter the path to the installation files.

4. Click the list arrow to select the modem you have previously installed.

5. Click the **OK** button.

6. Click the **Network** button and select the **TCP/IP** check box.

7. Click the **OK** button, and then click **OK** again.

8. Click the **Configure** button.

9. Verify that the **Dial Out Only** option button is selected.

10. Click the **OK** button.

11. Click the **Continue** button.

12. Click the **Yes** button when prompted to restart your computer.

Creating and configuring a RAS connection

1. Double-click the **My Computer** icon.

2. Double-click the **Dial-Up Networking** icon. If necessary, enter location information for your computer, click the **Close** button, and then double-click the **Dial-Up Networking** icon again.

3. Click the **OK** button.

4. Select the **I know all about phonebook entries** check box, and click the **Finish** button.

5. In the phone number box, type **555-5555**.

6. Click the **Server** tab.

7. Click the **TCP/IP Settings** button, and then click the **Specify name server addresses** option button.

8. Type **127.15.8.4** in the primary DNS box (this is a fictional DNS address).

9. Type **127.15.8.5** in the secondary DNS box (this is a fictional DNS address).

10. Click the **OK** button.

11. Click the **Security** tab.

12. Click the **Accept any authentication including clear text** option button.

13. Click the **OK** button.

Lab Notes

How do I uninstall RAS?—To uninstall RAS, access the Network icon via the Control Panel, and then click the Services tab. To completely remove RAS, select RAS by clicking on it and then clicking the Remove button.

Review Questions

Circle True or False.

1. Configuring a dialer in Windows 9x is the same as configuring a dialer in Windows NT.
   True / False

2. Windows NT will attempt to detect your modem after it has been installed. True / False

3. You use RAS to create and configure remote access connections. True / False

4. You can uninstall RAS by using the Add/Remove icon in the Control Panel. True / False

5. You can configure RAS to dial out or receive calls. True / False

6. A phone book entry is the Windows NT version of a dialer. True / False

7. Neil wants to configure his Windows NT computer to dial into the Internet but doesn't know where to type the DNS and WINS addresses. Describe where in Windows NT Neil must go to enter the DNS and WINS addresses for his remote connection.

   _____

   _____

   _____

   _____

   _____

15

LAB 15.4　MODEM TROUBLESHOOTING

Objective

The objective of this lab exercise is to provide you with hands-on practice troubleshooting Dial-Up Networking problems in both Windows 9x and Windows NT. After completing this lab exercise, you will be able to:

- Troubleshoot modem communications in Windows 9x.
- Troubleshoot modem communications in Windows NT.

Materials Required

This lab exercise requires one complete lab workstation for every four students. The lab workstations should meet the following requirements:

- 486 or better
- 16MB of RAM
- Windows 9x and Windows NT
- One internal modem

Lab Setup & Safety Tips

- Each lab workstation should be dual booted with the Windows 9x and Windows NT operating systems.
- During the following lab exercises, students are required to dial out using their modems. Note that an analog line for each lab workstation is not necessary. Students must be able to at least make the modem dial by clearing the Wait for dial tone before dialing check box. Note that this option is available in both Windows 9x and Windows NT.
- If students are working in pairs, designate one as Student 1 and the other as Student 2.

ACTIVITY

Troubleshooting modem communications in Windows 9x

The following steps should be performed while Student 2 is away from the lab workstation.

Student 1

1. Power on your lab workstation and allow it to boot into Windows 9x.
2. Click the **Start** button.
3. Point to **Settings**.
4. Click **Control Panel**.
5. Double-click the **System** icon.
6. Click the **Device Manager** tab.
7. Double-click the **Modem** icon.
8. Double-click the installed modem.
9. Clear the **Original Configuration** check box in Windows 95. In Windows 98, clear the **Disable in this hardware profile** check box.
10. Click the **OK** button.
11. Click the **Close** button.

12. Click the **Start** button.

13. Select the **Shut Down** option and restart the lab workstation.

Student 2

1. After Student 1 has reconfigured the lab workstation, answer the following questions and then repair the lab workstation. To repair your lab workstation, you must be able to create and dial out using a dialer configured with the TCP/IP protocol to use the following DNS numbers:

   Primary DNS: 15.8.457.1

   Secondary DNS: 15.8.245.6

   a. Are there any error messages? If so, write them down:

   _____

   _____

   b. What is the problem? Be specific.

   _____

   _____

   c. List several possible solutions.

   _____

   _____

   d. Test your theory (solution) and record the results.

   _____

   _____

   e. How did you discover the problem?

   _____

   _____

   _____

   f. What would you do differently in the future to improve your troubleshooting process?

   _____

   _____

   _____

   _____

Troubleshooting modem communications in Windows NT

Student 2

The following steps should be performed while Student 1 is away from the lab workstation.

1. Power on the lab workstation and allow it to boot into Windows NT.

2. Log on to Windows NT.

3. Click the **Start** button.

4. Point to **Settings**.

5. Click **Control Panel**.

6. Double-click the **Network** icon.

7. Click the **Services** tab.

8. Double-click **Remote Access Service**.

9. Click the **Network** button.

10. Clear the **TCP/IP** check box.

11. Select the **NetBeui** check box.

12. Click the **OK** button.

13. Click the **Continue** button.

14. If prompted, enter the path to the installation files.

15. Click the **Close** button.

16. Click the **Yes** button, and then restart the computer.

Student 1

1. After Student 2 has reconfigured the lab workstation, answer the following questions and then repair the lab workstation. To repair your lab workstation, you must be able to create and dial out using a phone book entry with the TCP/IP protocol configured to use the following DNS numbers:

   Primary DNS: 15.8.457.1

   Secondary DNS: 15.8.245.6

   a. Are there any error messages? If so, write them down:

   _____

   _____

   b. What is the problem? Be specific.

   _____

   _____

   c. List several possible solutions.

   _____

   _____

   d. Test your theory (solution) and record the results.

   _____

   _____

   e. How did you discover the problem?

   _____

   _____

   _____

f. What would you do differently in the future to improve your troubleshooting process?

_____

_____

_____

_____

> **Lab Notes**
>
> **What is ISDN?**—ISDN (Integrated Services Digital Network) is a communications standard that can carry digital data simultaneously over two channels on a single pair of wires at almost five times the speed of regular phone lines.

Review Questions

Circle True or False.

1. You can disable RAS by using the Modems option in the Control Panel. **True / False**

2. Windows 9x will allow you to create multiple phone book entries. **True / False**

3. In Windows 9x you can view a modem's resources by using the Device Manager. **True / False**

4. In Windows NT you can view a modem's resources by using the Device Manager. **True / False**

5. Peggy wants to reinstall RAS on her Windows NT computer. Describe how she could complete this task.

_____

_____

_____

_____

_____

6. Steve has decided to reinstall his modem driver on his Windows 9x computer. Describe the steps he should take to complete this task.

_____

_____

_____

_____

_____

15

NETWORKING FUNDAMENTALS AND THE INTERNET

LABS INCLUDED IN THIS CHAPTER

♦ LAB 16.1 NETWORK COMPONENT IDENTIFICATION

♦ LAB 16.2 NETWORKING AND WINDOWS 9x

♦ LAB 16.3 NETWORKING AND WINDOWS NT

♦ LAB 16.4 USING THE INTERNET

LAB 16.1 NETWORK COMPONENT IDENTIFICATION

Objective

The objective of this lab exercise is to install and configure a network interface card and to familiarize you with the common components of a networked environment. After completing this lab exercise, you will be able to:

- Install a network interface card.
- Identify some common networking components.
- Describe the functions of common networking components.

Materials Required

This lab exercise requires one complete lab workstation for every four students. The lab workstations should meet the following requirements:

- 486 or better
- 16MB of RAM
- Windows 9x

One network interface card for each lab workstation

This lab exercise also requires the following materials:

- DB-9 cable
- DB-25 cable
- One standard Centronics parallel cable
- RJ-25
- RJ-11
- RJ-14
- RJ-45
- BNC
- BNCT
- PS2/MINI-DIN
- ThickNet
- Unshielded twisted-pair wire
- Shielded twisted-pair wire
- One network interface card designed for use with both an RJ-45 connector and a BNC connector

If available for demonstration purposes, the instructor can use the following:

- One hub
- One router
- One switch
- Fiber-optic cable and connectors

The instructor also needs any of the following networking devices:

- Network sniffer

- Protocol analyzer

- Time domain reflector

- Any type of ISDN devices

Lab Setup & Safety Tips

- The instructor should label each network and wiring component.

- Students should follow grounding and ESD procedures.

- Always unplug the system unit before touching any component in the case.

ACTIVITY

Identifying network components

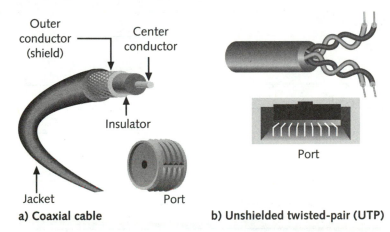

a) Coaxial cable   b) Unshielded twisted-pair (UTP)

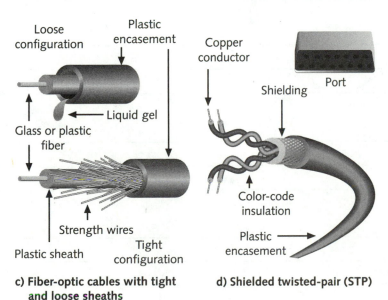

c) Fiber-optic cables with tight
   and loose sheaths   d) Shielded twisted-pair (STP)

Figure 16-1 Networking cables

16

1. Describe the function of each following component, and explain how it could be used in a networked environment.

    a. DB-9 cable

    _____

    _____

    _____

    b. DB-25 cable

    _____

    _____

    _____

    c. Centronics parallel data cable

    _____

    _____

    _____

    d. RJ-25

    _____

    _____

    _____

    e. RJ-11

    _____

    _____

    _____

    f. RJ-14

    _____

    _____

    _____

    g. RJ-45

    _____

    _____

    _____

    h. BNC

    _____

    _____

    _____

    i. BNCT

    _____

    _____

    _____

j. PS2/MINI-DIN

_____

_____

_____

k. ThickNet

_____

_____

_____

l. Unshielded twisted pair wire

_____

_____

_____

m. Shielded twisted pair wire

_____

_____

_____

n. Network interface card

_____

_____

_____

o. Hub

_____

_____

_____

p. Router

_____

_____

_____

q. Switch

_____

_____

_____

r. Fiber optics

_____

_____

_____

16

s. Network sniffer

_____

_____

_____

t. Protocol analyzer

_____

_____

_____

u. Time domain reflector

_____

_____

_____

v. ISDN devices

_____

_____

_____

Installing the network interface card

1. Unplug the power cord.

2. Remove the case.

3. Locate an available slot where you will install the network interface card.

4. Using the documentation provided, verify that the network interface card is configured to use the predetermined I/O address and has an available IRQ.

5. Gently install the network interface card into the slot. *Warning*: Don't bend the card from side to side; move the card only back and forth from end to end.

6. Screw the mounting screw into place.

7. Replace the top of the case.

8. Plug in the system unit.

9. Power on the lab workstation and allow it to boot into Windows 9x.

10. If the workstation fails to boot properly, power cycle the PC, and when prompted, choose Safe Mode.

Lab Notes

What does RJ stand for?—RJ stands for registered jack.

What does LAN stand for?—The term LAN stands for local area network. LAN normally refers to a small or midsized network that is contained within a small geographical area.

What does WAN stand for?—The term WAN stands for wide area network. WAN normally refers to a network that is spread across a large geographical area.

What is a MAN?—The term MAN stands for metropolitan area network. MAN is normally used to refer to a small or midsized network that is contained within a metropolitan area.

A+ CERTIFICATION OBJECTIVES

Table 16-1   Core A+ Objectives

Objectives	Chapters	Page Numbers
1.3 Identify available IRQs, DMAs, and I/O addresses and procedures for configuring them for device installation.	2, 5, 7, 9	
A. Standard IRQ settings	2, 9	83, 90, 463
1.4 Identify common peripheral ports, associated cabling, and their connectors.	1, 9, 15, 16	
A. Cable types	1	19
B. Cable orientation	9	462
C. Serial versus parallel	1, 9	19, 463, 469-471
D. Pin connections	9, 15, 16	
1. DB-9	9	462
2. DB-25	9	462
3. RJ-11	15	804
4. RJ-45	16	861-864
5. BNC	16	861-864
6. PS2/MINI-DIN	9	487-488
5.3 Identify the types of printer connections and configurations.	9, 17	
A. Parallel	9	469-471
B. Serial	9	462, 463
C. Network	17	956-959
7.1 Identify basic networking concepts, including how a network works.	15, 16	
A. Network access	16	861-864, 875-877
C. Network Interface Cards	16	869-872
D. Full-duplex	15	804
E. Cabling: Twisted Pair, Coaxial, Fiber Optic	16	861-864
F. Ways to network a PC	16	861-864, 877, 878, 883, 884
7.2 Identify procedures for swapping and configuring network interface cards.	16	886-889

16

Review Questions

Circle True or False.

1. An RJ-11 connector is commonly used as telephone wire.   True / False

2. RJ stands for registered jack.   True / False

3. RJ-45 connectors are often used in a LAN environment.   True / False

4. BNC connectors are most commonly used to connect UTP.   True / False

5. Describe the difference between UTP and STP.

_____

_____

_____

_____

_____

6. Describe the difference between a router and a hub.

_____

_____

_____

_____

_____

LAB 16.2 NETWORKING AND WINDOWS 9X

Objective

The objective of this lab exercise is to provide you with hands-on networking experience in the Windows 9x environment. After completing this lab exercise, you will be able to:

- Install network interface card drivers.
- Configure Windows 9x to communicate on a LAN.
- Share resources in a networked environment.
- Map a network drive.
- Configure the TCP/IP protocol in the Windows 9x environment.

Materials Required

This lab exercise requires one complete lab workstation for every four students. The lab workstations should meet the following requirements:

- 486 or better
- 16MB of RAM
- Windows 9x
- One network interface card

Lab Setup & Safety Tips

- Each lab workstation should have Windows 9x installed and functioning properly.
- Each lab workstation should have one network interface card installed.
- The classroom should be wired for network communications.
- The instructor will provide an IP address for each lab workstation prior to the start of activities. *Note*: All IP addresses issued should be on the same subnet unless the classroom supports other configurations.
- The instructor will provide computer names for each lab workstation before the activities are completed.

ACTIVITY

Installing network interface card drivers

The following lab exercise assumes that your lab workstation is not configured with any networking components. If your lab workstation does have networking components installed, remove them all, and reboot your system before proceeding.

1. Power on your lab workstation and allow it to boot into Windows 9x.
2. Click the **Start** button.
3. Point to **Settings**.
4. Click **Control Panel**.
5. Double-click the **Network** icon.
6. Click the **Add** button.
7. In the list of network components, double-click **Client**.

16

8. In the list of manufacturers, click **Microsoft**.

9. In the list of network clients, double-click **Client for Microsoft Networks**.

10. In the list of manufacturers, click **NIC**.

11. Double-click the correct NIC driver.

12. Click the **Add** button.

13. Double-click the **Protocol** option.

14. In the Manufacturers list, click **Microsoft**.

15. Double-click the **TCP/IP** option.

16. Click the **Identification** tab.

17. Type the computer name specified by your instructor.

18. Click the **OK** button.

19. If prompted, enter the path to the installation files.

20. Click the **Yes** button when you are prompted to restart your computer.

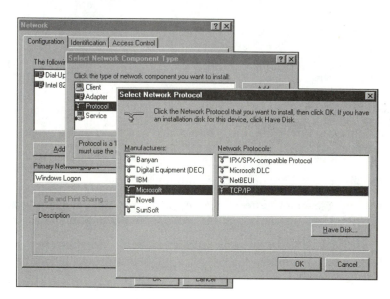

Figure 16-2   Installing TCP/IP for Windows 95 using the
Control Panel

Configuring the TCP/IP protocol

1. Click the **Start** button.

2. Point to **Settings**.

3. Click **Control Panel**.

4. Double-click the **Network** icon.

5. Double-click the **TCP/IP** protocol.

6. Click the **Specify an IP address** option button.

7. Type the IP address issued to your lab workstation.

8. Enter any additional information your instructor requires.

9. Click the **OK** button to close the TCP/IP Properties dialog box.

10. Click the **OK** button to close the Network dialog box.

11. Click the **Yes** button when prompted to restart your computer.

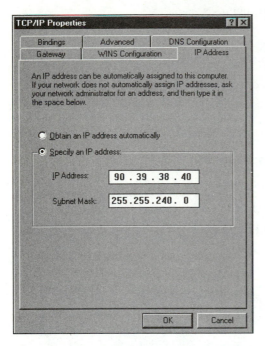

Figure 16-3   Configuring TCP/IP for Windows 9x static IP
addressing

Using the PING command to test the network

1. Click the **Start** button.

2. Point to **Programs**.

3. Click **MS-DOS Prompt**.

4. Type **PING** ###.###.###.### (### represents your lab workstation's IP address).

5. Type **PING** ###.###.###.### (### represents the IP address of your neighbor's lab workstation).

Enabling resource sharing

1. Click the **Start** button.

2. Point to **Settings**.

3. Click **Control Panel**.

4. Double-click the **Network** icon.

5. Click the **File and Printer Sharing** button.

6. Click both check boxes to check them and allow the lab workstations to share resources.

7. Click the **OK** button to close the File and Printer Sharing dialog box.

8. Click the **OK** button to close the Network dialog box.

9. Click the **Yes** button when prompted to restart your computer.

16

Sharing your C drive

1. Double-click the **My Computer** icon.

2. Right-click the icon for your C drive.

3. Select **Properties** from the shortcut menu.

4. Click the **Sharing** tab.

5. Click the **Shared As** option button.

6. Click the **Full** option button.

7. Click the **OK** button.

Connecting to a shared resource

1. Right-click the **Network Neighborhood** icon.

2. Select the **Map Network Drive** option.

3. Click the Drive list arrow and then click the drive letter **G**.

4. Type *COMPUTERNAME\SHARENAME* in the path box (the computer and share name should be your neighbor's).

5. Click the **OK** button.

Lab Notes

What is a protocol?—A protocol is a language computers use to communicate in a networked environment.

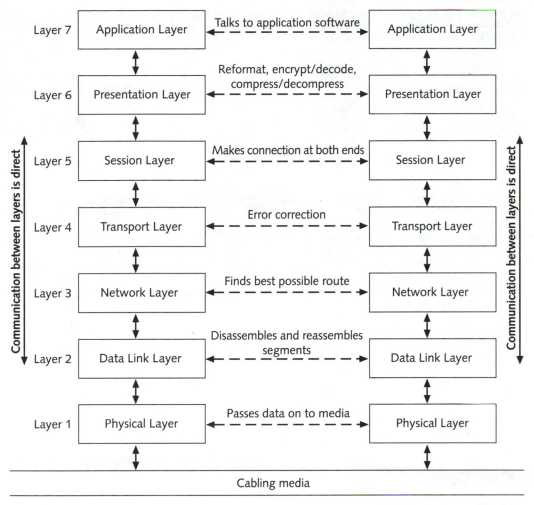

Figure 16-4   The OSI reference model identifies seven layers of network communication within software and firmware

Lab Notes

What is bandwidth?—In the networking environment, bandwidth refers to the amount of data that can travel through a wire at any one time.

What is a gateway?—A gateway is a device or process that connects networks with different protocols. A router often is used as a gateway.

What is DNS?—DNS stands for Domain Name System or Domain Name Service. A DNS is a database on a top-level domain name server that keeps track of assigned domain names and their corresponding IP addresses.

CERTIFICATION OBJECTIVES

Table 16-2   DOS/Windows A+ Objectives

Objectives	Chapters	Page Numbers
5.1 Identify the networking capabilities of DOS and Windows including procedures for connecting to the network.	16, 17	
A. Sharing disk drives	16	883, 884, 920-925
B. Sharing print and file services	16, 17	886-889, 956
C. Network type and network card	16	869-872

Table 16-3   Core A+ Objectives

Objectives	Chapters	Page Numbers
7.1 Identify basic networking concepts, including how a network works.	15, 16	
A. Network access	16	861-864, 875-877
B. Protocol	16	861-864, 874, 875
C. Network Interface Cards	16	869-872
F. Ways to network a PC	16	861-864, 877, 878, 883, 884
7.3 Identify the ramifications of repairs on the network.	16	
A. Reduced bandwidth	16	861-864
B. Loss of data	16	861-864
C. Network slowdown	16	861-864

Review Questions

Circle True or False.

1. You can configure Windows 9x to use an IP address by using the Control Panel Network option. True / False

2. You can use the PING command to share network resources.   True / False

3. All network drives that map from a Windows 9x PC to a Windows 9x PC must be mapped as drive G.   True / False

4. Melanie accesses her network properties on her Windows 9x computer by right-clicking the My Computer icon and selecting Properties from the shortcut menu.   True / False

5. Roy wants to enable file and printer sharing on his Windows 9x laptop. He has already installed TCP/IP and can share resources on the network, but is unable to share any files. Describe the steps that Roy should take to enable file and printer sharing.

_____

_____

_____

_____

_____

6. Where do you specify a computer and workgroup name in Windows 9x?

_____

_____

_____

_____

_____

16

LAB 16.3 NETWORKING AND WINDOWS NT

Objective

The objective of this lab exercise is to provide you with hands-on networking experience in the Windows NT environment. After completing this lab exercise, you will be able to:

- Install network interface card drivers.
- Configure Windows NT workstation to communicate on a LAN.
- Share resources in a networked environment.
- Map a network drive in the Windows NT environment.
- Configure the TCP/IP protocol in the Windows NT environment.

Materials Required

This lab exercise requires one complete lab workstation for every four students. The lab workstations should meet the following requirements:

- 486 or better
- 16MB of RAM
- Windows NT
- One Network Interface card (must be NT compatible)

Lab Setup & Safety Tips

- The classroom should be wired for network communications.
- Each lab workstation should have Windows NT installed and functioning properly.
- Each lab workstation should have one network interface card installed.
- The instructor will provide an IP address for each lab workstation prior to the start of activities. *Note*: All IP addresses should be on the same subnet unless the classroom supports other configurations.
- The instructor will provide computer names to each lab workstation before the activities are completed.

ACTIVITY

Installing network interface card drivers and configuring TCP/IP

1. Power on your lab workstation and allow it to boot into the Windows NT environment.
2. Click the **Start** button.
3. Point to **Settings**.
4. Click **Control Panel**.
5. Double-click the **Network** icon.
6. Click the **Adapter** tab.
7. Click the **Add** button.
8. Select the correct NIC driver from the list.
9. Click the **OK** button.
10. If prompted, enter the path to the installation files.
11. Click the **Protocol** tab.

12. Click the **Add** button.

13. Select **TCP/IP Protocol** from the list provided.

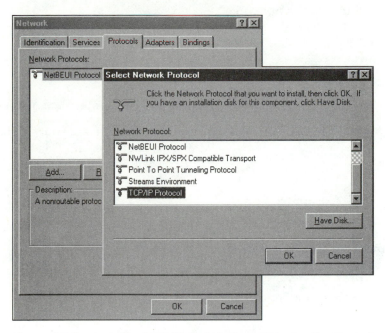

Figure 16-5   Installing TCP/IP for Windows NT using the Control Panel

14. Click the **OK** button. If you see a message asking if you want to use dynamic binding, click **No**.

15. In the Protocol list, click **TCP/IP**, and then click the **Properties** button.

16. Type the IP address issued to your lab workstation.

17. Enter any additional information your instructor requires.

16

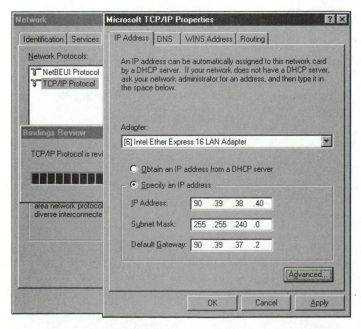

Figure 16-6   Configuring TCP/IP for Windows NT for static IP addressing

18. Click the **Close** button.

19. Click the **Yes** button when prompted to restart your computer.

Using the PING command to test the network

1. Click the **Start** button.

2. Point to **Programs**.

3. Click **MS-DOS Prompt**.

4. Type **PING** ###.###.###.### (### represents your lab workstation's IP address).

5. Type **PING** ###.###.###.### (### represents the IP address of your neighbor's lab workstation).

Sharing your C drive

1. Double-click the **My Computer** icon.

2. Right-click the icon for your C drive.

3. Select **Properties** from the shortcut menu.

4. Click the **Sharing** tab.

5. Click the **Not Shared** option button.

6. Click the **Apply** button.

7. Click the **Shared As** option button.

8. Click the **OK** button.

Connecting to a shared resource

1. Right-click the **Network Neighborhood** icon.

2. Select the **Map Network Drive** option.

3. Click the Drive drop-down arrow and choose the drive letter **G**, if available.

4. Type *COMPUTERNAME\SHARENAME* in the path box (the computer and share name should be your neighbor's).

5. Click the **OK** button.

Lab Notes

How is the default gateway used?—The client uses the default gateway to send data packets to an IP address on a different network.

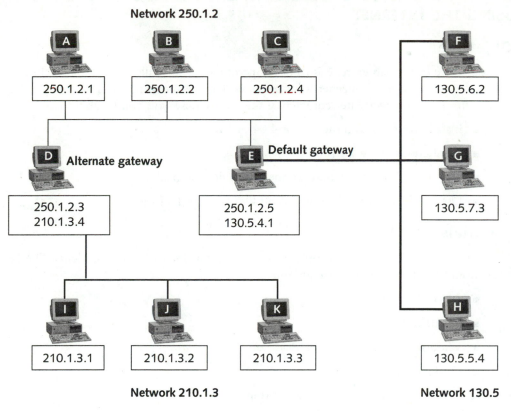

Figure 16-7   A network can have more than one router. One router of the network will
be the default gateway

Review Questions

Circle True or False.

1. Windows NT does not allow you to share your C drive.   True / False

2. The PING command serves the same function in both Windows 9x and Windows NT.
True / False

3. To install a protocol in the Windows NT environment, you must view the Network properties,
choose the Protocol tab, and click the Add button.   True / False

4. Roxy wants to change her Windows NT computer name. To complete this task, Roxy
opens the Network properties window and chooses the Bindings tab. True / False

5. Windows NT allows you to share and connect to different network resources.   True / False

6. Max wants to connect his Windows NT computer to a UNIX share. Max wants the UNIX
share to appear as drive N in his My Computer window. Describe the steps Max will take to
map a UNIX share as his network drive N.

_____

_____

_____

_____

_____

16

LAB 16.4 USING THE INTERNET

Objective

The objective of this lab exercise is to develop your Internet skills. These skills include the installation and configuration of Internet software, as well as the browsing for and downloading of information from the Internet. After completing this lab exercise, you will be able to:

- Install Netscape Communicator 4.04 or later.

- Configure a Netscape profile.

- Use the HTTP protocol to connect and view Web sites.

- Use the FTP protocol to download files from an FTP site.

Materials Required

This lab exercise requires one complete lab workstation for every four students. The lab workstations should meet the following requirements:

- 486 or better

- 16MB of RAM

- Windows 9x

- One modem

Netscape Communicator 4.04 standard edition or later

Lab Setup & Safety Tips

- Each lab workstation should have access to the Internet and have Windows 9x installed and functioning properly.

- Each lab workstation should have the Netscape Communicator installation files on drive C before starting the activity.

ACTIVITY

Installing Netscape Communicator 4.04 standard edition

Note: The following steps have been tested and verified as accurate for Netscape Communicator 4.04. Steps may vary for other versions of Netscape Communicator.

1. Power on your lab workstation and allow it to boot into Windows 9x.

2. Double-click the **Netscape Installation** icon to start the Setup program.

3. Click the **Next** button.

4. Click the **Yes** button.

5. Click the **Next** button.

6. Click the **Yes** button.

7. Click the **Next** button.

8. Click the **Install** button.

9. Click the **No** button.

10. Click the **OK** button.

Configuring your Netscape profile

1. Click the **Start** button.

2. Point to **Programs**.

3. Point to **Netscape Communicator**.

4. Click the **Netscape Messenger** icon.

5. Click the **Next** button.

6. Type *your name* in the Full Name box.

7. Type *your e-mail address* in the Email address box.

8. Click the **Next** button.

9. Type *your name* in the Profile Name box.

10. Click the **Next** button.

11. Type the name of your SMTP server in the Outgoing Mail (SMTP) Server box.

12. Click the **Next** button.

13. Type your mail server user name in the Mail Server User Name box.

14. Type the name of your POP or IMAP server in the Incoming Mail Server box.

15. Click the correct option button to specify either a POP3 server or an IMAP server.

16. Click the **Next** button.

17. Type the name of your news server in the News (NNTP) server box.

18. Click the **Finish** button.

19. Click the **Do not perform this check in the future** check box to select it.

20. Click the **Yes** button.

21. Close Netscape Messenger.

Using the HTTP protocol

1. If necessary, connect to the Internet.

2. Launch Netscape Communicator.

3. In the location box, type **WWW.MICROSOFT.COM**.

4. Press **Enter**.

Using the FTP protocol

1. Launch Netscape Communicator.

2. In the location box, type **ftp://ftp.intel.com**.

3. Click the **Readme** link to see the readme file.

16

Configuring Netscape Communicator browser to use a proxy server

In the following section you will configure your Web browser to use to use a sample proxy server for the HTTP and FTP services called WEB-PROXY.LAB.TEST.COM:8088.

1. Launch Netscape Communicator.

2. Click the **Edit** menu.

3. Click **Preferences**.

4. In the Category text box, click the **Advanced** option.

5. Click **Proxies**.

6. Click the **Manual Proxy configuration** option button.

7. Click the **View** button.

8. In the HTTP box, type **WEB-PROXY.LAB.TEST.COM**, press Tab, and type **8088**.

9. In the FTP box, type **WEB-PROXY.LAB.TEST.COM**, press Tab, and type **8088**.

10. Click the **OK** button.

11. Click the **OK** button.

>
> ## Lab Notes
> **What is an ISP?**—ISP stands for Internet Service Provider. ISPs are used as connection points to the Internet. When at home, most people dial into an ISP network that is connected to the Internet. This gives home users access to the Internet.

 ## CERTIFICATION OBJECTIVES

Table 16-4   DOS/Windows A+ Objectives

Objectives	Chapters	Page Numbers
5.2 Identify concepts and capabilities relating to the Internet and basic procedures for setting up a system for Internet access.	16, 18	
A. TCP/IP	16	893, 896
B. E-mail	18	984
C. HTML	16	916, 917
D. HTTP://	16	916, 917
E. FTP	16	917, 918
F Domain Names (Web sites)	16	899
H. Dial-up access	16	879-882, 912-915

Review Questions

Circle True or False.

1. Netscape Communicator is a Web server software package.   True / False

2. The HTTP protocol is used when viewing Web pages like www.microsoft.com.   True / False

3. You can download a file from the Internet by clicking the link to the file and pressing the Save button.   True / False

4. Netscape Communicator does not support proxy servers.   True / False

5. Describe the steps you take to connect to an FTP site.

   _____

   _____

   _____

   _____

   _____

6. List three examples of domain names.

   _____

   _____

   _____

   _____

   _____

16

CHAPTER

17

PRINTERS

Lab 17.1 Understanding Laser Printers

Objective

The objective of this lab exercise is for you to inspect and understand the function of each component within a laser printer. After completing this lab exercise, you will be able to:

- Describe the function of each internal laser printer component.
- Describe the laser printing process.

Materials Required

This lab exercise requires one complete lab workstation for every four students. The lab workstation should meet the following requirements:

- 486 or better
- 16MB of RAM
- Windows 9x

One functional laser printer for each lab workstation

One disassembled printer cartridge

Labels for each lab laser printer

Lab Setup & Safety Tips

- Each lab workstation should have Windows 9x installed and functioning properly.
- The instructor should be familiar with the lab laser printers.
- Students must comply with standard ESD procedures.
- Always unplug the power cord before touching any component in the printer.

Activity

Inspecting and labeling a laser printer cartridge

1. Using the figure below, identify each component in the disassembled laser printer cartridge, and describe its function on the lines provided.

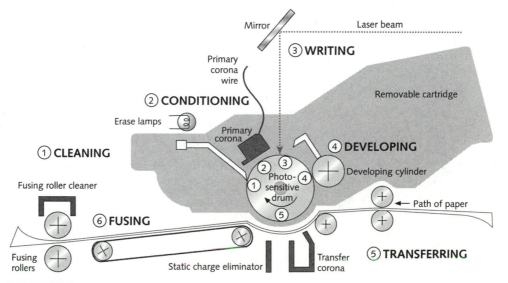

Figure 17-1   The six progressive steps of laser printing

Primary corona

_____

_____

_____

Photo-sensitive drum

_____

_____

_____

Developing cylinder

_____

_____

_____

Inspecting and labeling a laser printer

Although all laser printers follow the same printing process, each has a different design. Your instructor will show you how to disassemble your lab workstation's laser printer so you can complete the following exercise.

1. Power off and unplug your laser printer.

   (If your laser printer has been used recently, allow it to cool before proceeding.)

2. Open your laser printer.

3. Identify each of the following laser printer components and describe its functionality:

   Fuser

   _____

   _____

   _____

   Paper tray

   _____

   _____

   _____

   Primary corona wire

   _____

   _____

   _____

   Transfer corona

   _____

   _____

   _____

17

Power supply

_____

_____

_____

Sensors (all)

_____

_____

_____

Expansion slots

_____

_____

_____

Logic boards (all)

_____

_____

_____

Lab Notes

The Six Steps of Laser Printing:

Step 1: Cleaning

The printer uses the cleaning blade to scrape leftover toner from the previous image off the drum. It removes the previous electrostatic image from the drum with an erase lamp.

Step 2: Conditioning

The primary corona applies a uniform negative charge (-600 volts) to prepare the drum for the new image. *Warning:* Do not expose the drum to light.

Step 3: Writing

- The PC sends the image to the formatter.
- The PC formatter sends the image to the DC controller.
- A laser beam is initiated and directed toward the scanning mirror.
- The laser beam reflects off the scanning mirror and is focused by the focusing lens.
- The laser deflects off the mirror and is projected through a slit into the removable cartridge.

Note that the speed of both the drum motor and the scanning mirror motor are synchronized so that the laser beam completes one scanline and returns to the beginning of the drum.

Step 4: Developing

The electrostatic image develops into a visible image when toner from a developer cylinder is transferred to the discharged (-100 volt) areas of the drum. The developer cylinder has a magnetic core that attracts the iron in the toner. As the cylinder rotates, the doctor blade keeps the toner at a uniform height. The toner acquires a negative charge by rubbing against the developer cylinder. This negative charge causes the toner to be attracted to the relatively positive (-100 volt) areas of the drum that have been exposed to the laser light.

Lab Notes (continued)

Step 5: Transferring

The transfer corona produces a positive charge (+600 volts) on the back of the paper that pulls the toner off the drum and onto the paper. Once the toner is on the paper, a static charge eliminator reduces the paper's charge.

Step 6: Fusing

The toner is held on the paper by gravity and a weak electrostatic charge until it reaches the fuser assembly. Heat (180° C/356° F) and pressure applied by the fuser rollers melt the toner into the paper and produce a permanent image. Because the photo-sensitive drum is 3.75 inches in circumference, the print cycle must be repeated several times to print one sheet of paper. If the temperature rises above 410° F, the printer automatically shuts down to cool off the fuser.

What about ink jet printers?

As the print head moves across the paper, an electrical pulse flows through thin resistors at the bottom of all the chambers that the printer uses to form a character or image. The resistor in each chamber heats a thin layer of ink to more than 900° F to form a vapor bubble. As the vapor bubble expands, it pushes ink through the nozzle to transfer a drop of ink to the paper. A typical character is formed by an array of ink drops 20 across by 20 high.

CERTIFICATION OBJECTIVES

Table 17-1   Core A+ Objectives

Objectives	Chapters	Page Numbers
3.3 Identify the potential hazards and proper safety procedures relating to lasers and high-voltage equipment.	11, 18	
A. Lasers	18	981
B. High-voltage equipment	11	573
C. Power supply	11	573
5.1 Identify basic concepts, printer operations and printer components.	8, 17	
A. Types of Printers	8, 17	
1. Laser	8, 17	435-439, 940-945
2. Inkjet	17	946-948
3. Dot Matrix	8, 17	941-945
B. Paper feeder mechanisms	17	941-945
5.2 Identify care and service techniques and common problems with primary printer types.	8, 17, Appendix E	
A. Feed and output	8	435-439
B. Errors	8, Appendix E	435-439, E17-E19
C. Paper jam	8	435-439
D. Print quality	8, Appendix E	435-439, E20
E. Safety precautions	17	948
F. Preventive maintenance	17	948

17

Review Questions

Circle True or False.

1. The photo-sensitive drum is always housed within the printer cartridge.   True / False

2. The primary corona is always housed within the fuser.   True / False

3. The erase lamp melts excess ink off the photo-sensitive drum.   True / False

4. During the printing process, mirrors are used to control the movement of a tiny laser beam.   True / False

5. The primary corona wire is a small wire that should be attached between the primary corona and fuser.   True / False

6. All laser printers use only one motor.   True / False

7. What are the six steps of the laser printing process?

_____

_____

_____

_____

_____

8. Describe how to replace the fuser in your lab workstation.

_____

_____

_____

_____

_____

LAB 17.2 INSTALLING AND SHARING LOCAL PRINTERS

Objective

The objective of this lab exercise is to install a printer, load the proper drivers, and share the printer on the network. After completing this lab exercise, you will be able to:

- Install a local printer.
- Install printer drivers.
- Share a local printer.

Materials Required

This lab exercise requires one complete lab workstation for every four students. The lab workstation should meet the following requirements:

- 486 or better
- 16MB of RAM
- Windows 9x
- One CD-ROM drive

One functional laser printer for each lab workstation

The cords and cables necessary to connect each laser printer to its respective lab workstation

One Windows 9x CD for each lab workstation

Lab Setup & Safety Tips

- Each lab workstation should have Windows 9x installed and functioning properly.
- Each lab workstation should be configured to communicate on the network.
- The instructor should be familiar with the lab laser printers.

ACTIVITY

Installing a Local Printer

1. Power off your lab workstation.
2. Locate the parallel cable for your printer.
3. Attach the appropriate end of the cable to the back of the printer.
4. Attach the other end of the cable to the back of your lab workstation.
5. Plug in the power cord for the printer.
6. Power on your lab workstation and allow it to boot into Windows 9x.

Installing a printer driver

1. Double-click the **My Computer** icon.
2. Double-click the **Printers** folder.
3. Double-click **Add Printer**.
4. Click the **Next** button.
5. Choose the **My Computer** option, and click the **Next** button.

17

6. Choose whether you want to install a local or networked printer. Then choose the correct printer driver by selecting the appropriate manufacturer and the printer model. Click the **OK** button when you are done.

7. Select the appropriate printer port, and click the **Next** button.

8. In the Printer Name text box type **PRINTER1**.

9. Click the **Yes** toggle button to select this printer as your Windows default.

10. Click the **Next** button.

11. Click the **Yes** toggle button and then click the **Finish** button to print a test page.

12. Close the Printers folder by clicking the **Close** button (**X** in the upper-right corner of the window).

13. Close the My Computer window by clicking the **Close** button (**X** in the upper-right corner of the window).

Installing file and print sharing for Windows 9x

1. Click the **Start** button, point to **Settings**, and choose **Control Panel**.

2. Double-click the **Network** icon.

3. On the **Configuration** tab, click the **File and Print Sharing** button.

4. In the File and Print Sharing window, click the **I want to be able to allow others to print to my printer(s)** check box.

5. Click the **OK** button.

6. Click the **Next** button in the Network Properties window.

7. Insert the Windows 9x CD if prompted, and then click **OK**.

8. Click **Yes** when prompted to restart your computer.

Sharing a local printer

1. Click the **Start** button, point to **Settings**, and then click **Printers**.

2. In the Printers window, right-click the **PRINTER1** print object.

3. Choose **Properties** from the shortcut menu.

4. Click the **Sharing** tab.

5. Click the **Shared As** option button.

6. Notice that the printer name (in this case PRINTER1) has appeared in the Share Name text box. Use this text box to change the name that a printer is shared as, and the printer doesn't have to be renamed.

7. Click the **OK** button to begin sharing the printer.

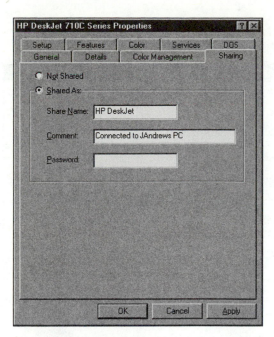

Figure 17-2   Using Windows 98 to share a connected printer with other computers on the network

 Lab Notes

Are serial connections used with printers?—Although serial connections are becoming obsolete, some printers still provide backward compatibility for such use. If a printer does not provide support for serial connections, you might be required to purchase a serial expansion card.

How do I fix a paper jam?—If paper becomes jammed inside a printer, find the location of the paper jam and pull gently and evenly to remove the paper. Always check the printer documentation for specifics before you clear a paper jam.

How do I prevent white streaks from appearing when I print a document?— When streaks or speckles appear on documents, you first check your print cartridge. Remove the cartridge and then tap or gently shake the toner cartridge to redistribute the toner. If the problem persists, check the printer manual for specific parts that may need attention.

What about preventive maintenance?—Check the documentation provided with the printer. Some manufacturers sell PM kits (Preventive Maintenance kits) which include the parts that receive the most wear and tear.

17

CERTIFICATION OBJECTIVES

A+

Table 17-2   Core A+ Objectives

Objectives	Chapters	Page Numbers
5.1 Identify basic concepts, printer operations and printer components.	8, 17	
A. Types of Printers	8, 17	
1. Laser	8, 17	435-439, 940-945
2. Inkjet	17	946-948
3. Dot Matrix	8, 17	438, 949
5.3 Identify the types of printer connections and configurations.	9, 17	
A. Parallel	9	469-471
B. Serial	9	462, 463
C. Network	17	956-959
5.2 Identify care and service techniques and common problems with primary printer types.	8, 17, Appendix E	
A. Feed and output	8	435-439
B. Errors	8, Appendix E	435-439, E17-E19
C. Paper jam	8	435-439
D. Print quality	8, Appendix E	435-439, E20
E. Safety precautions	17	948
F. Preventive maintenance	17	948

Table 17-3   DOS/Windows A+ Objectives

Objectives	Chapters	Page Numbers
3.4 Identify procedures for loading/adding device drivers and the necessary software for certain devices.	4, 9, 10	
A. Windows 3.x procedures	4	198, 199
B. Windows 95 Plug and Play	9, 10	459-461, 526

Review Questions

Circle True or False.

1. You can use either a serial or parallel cable to connect to some printers.   True / False

2. Parallel printing is faster than serial printing.   True / False

3. You can enable File and Print Sharing in Windows 9x by double-clicking the Network icon in the Control panel to open the Network dialog box.   True / False

4. In Windows 9x, you first must install File and Print Sharing to allow other people to print to your local printer.   True / False

5. You install printer drivers using the Add New Hardware icon in the Control Panel.   True / False

6. Angie is trying to share her local printer so Bart can print to it. When she views the properties of the installed printer, she doesn't see a Sharing tab. Explain why Angie doesn't have a Sharing tab for her printer and describe the steps she needs to take to share her printer with Bart.

_____

_____

_____

_____

_____

17

LAB 17.3 TROUBLESHOOTING SHARED PRINTERS

Objective

The objective of this lab exercise is to give you experience both in printing to a network printer and troubleshooting printing in a networked environment. After completing this lab exercise, you will be able to:

- Connect to a shared printer.
- Print to a shared printer.
- Troubleshoot network printing.

Materials Required

This lab exercise requires one complete lab workstation for every two students. The lab workstation should meet the following requirements:

- 486 or better
- 16MB of RAM
- Windows 9x

One functional laser printer for each lab workstation

The cords and cables necessary to connect each laser printer to its respective lab workstation

Lab Setup & Safety Tips

- Each lab workstation should have Windows 9x installed and functioning properly.
- Each lab workstation should be configured to communicate on the network.
- The instructor and students should be familiar with the lab laser printers.
- Each lab workstation should be configured so a local laser printer can be installed correctly and shared on the network as Printer1.
- The instructor should designate groups, two pairs of students to a group.
- Each pair of students will assume a role, Student 1 or Student 2.

ACTIVITY

Connecting to a Shared Printer

Student 1

1. Power on your lab workstation and allow it to boot into Windows 9x.
2. Click the **Start** button, point to **Settings**, and then click **Control Panel**.
3. Double-click the **Network** icon and then use the Identification tab to identify Student 2's lab workstation.
4. Click the **Start** button, point to **Settings**, and then click **Printers**.
5. Double-click the **Add Printer** icon and then click the **Next** button.
6. Click the **Network Printer** option button.
7. Click the **Next** button.
8. In the **Network printer or queue name** text box, type *Student 2's computer name***Printer1**.

9. Click the **Next** button.

10. If both lab workstations are using the same operating system, the printer driver will automatically be installed. You then can click the **Finish** button. If this isn't the case, complete Steps 11–12.

11. From the list, choose the appropriate manufacturer and printer type, and then click the **Next** button.

12. Click the **Finish** button.

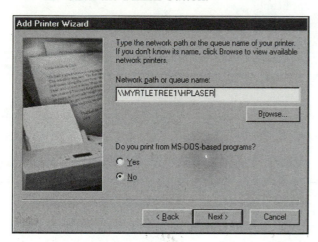

Figure 17-3   Setting up a network printer in Windows 9x

Creating problem 1

Student 2

While Student 1 is away from the workstation, proceed with the following steps:

1. Click the **Start** button, point to **Settings**, and then click **Printers**.

2. Click the **PRINTER1** icon.

3. Click the **File** menu.

4. Click the **Work offline** option to check it.

5. Close the Printer window.

Troubleshooting and resolving problem 1

Student 1

After Student 2 has reconfigured one or both of the lab workstations, answer the following questions and repair the network printing function.

Are there any error messages? If so, write them down.

_____

_____

_____

_____

_____

17

What is the problem? Be specific.

_____

_____

_____

_____

_____

List several possible solutions (if applicable).

_____

_____

_____

_____

_____

Test your theory (solution) and record the results.

_____

_____

_____

_____

_____

How did you discover the problem?

_____

_____

_____

_____

_____

What would you do differently in the future to improve your troubleshooting process?

_____

_____

_____

_____

_____

Creating problem 2

Student 1

While Student 2 is away from the workstation, proceed with the following steps on Student 2's lab workstation:

1. Click the **Start** button, point to **Settings**, and then click **Printers**.

2. Right-click the **PRINTER1** icon and choose **Sharing** from the shortcut menu.

3. In the **Share Name** text box, type **PRINTER2**.

4. Click the **Apply** button.

5. Click the **OK** button.

6. Click the **OK** button.

7. Close the Printer window.

Troubleshooting and resolving problem 2

Student 2

After Student 2 has reconfigured one or both of the lab workstations, answer the following questions and repair the network printing function.

Are there any error messages? If so, write them down.

_____

_____

_____

_____

_____

What is the problem? Be specific.

_____

_____

_____

_____

_____

List several possible solutions (if applicable).

_____

_____

_____

_____

_____

Test your theory (solution) and record the results.

_____

_____

_____

_____

_____

How did you discover the problem?

_____

_____

_____

_____

What would you do differently in the future to improve your troubleshooting process?

_____

_____

_____

_____

_____

17

Lab Notes

Can I share my C drive like I share a printer?—Yes. Sharing your C drive is similar to sharing a printer. First you must use the Network applet in the Control Panel to enable the File Sharing service. Next, locate the directory or drive that you want to share, and then click the Sharing tab on the Network Properties sheet to configure drive sharing service.

What is the Work Offline setting used for?—The Work Offline feature in Windows 9x is designed for users that are not always connected to a network or a printer. When you select the Work Offline feature, Windows allows you to spool print jobs, but will not attempt to print them until you deselect Work Offline. This allows remote users to print a document the next time a printer becomes available.

 ## CERTIFICATION OBJECTIVES

Table 17-4   Core A+ Objectives

Objectives	Chapters	Page Numbers
5.1 Identify basic concepts, printer operations and printer components.	8, 17	
A. Types of Printers	8, 17	
1. Laser	8, 17	435-439, 940-945
2. Inkjet	17	946-948
3. Dot Matrix	8, 17	438, 949

Table 17-5   DOS/Windows A+ Objectives

Objectives	Chapters	Page Numbers
3.5 Identify the procedures for changing options, configuring, and using the Windows printing subsystem.	17	
4.2 Recognize Windows-specific printing problems and identify the procedures for correcting them.	17	
A. Print spool is stalled	17	950
B. Incorrect/incompatible driver for print	17	951-955
5.1 Identify the networking capabilities of DOS and Windows including procedures for connecting to the network.	16, 17	
A. Sharing disk drives	16	883, 884, 920-925
B. Sharing print and file services	16, 17	886-889, 956

Review Questions

Circle **True** or **False**.

1. When connecting to a shared printer you always must be installed locally.   True / False

2. When a device is configured to work offline, it will queue print jobs, but will not attempt to print them until it is brought back online.   True / False

3. A printer's share name is always the same as the printer name.   True / False

4. UNC syntax is typically used when mapping to a shared print device.   True / False

5. Jacob has shared an HP LaserJet 4 printer on the network. Jacob gave you the following information and told you to set up the printer on your workstation.

   Computer Name: Jacob1

   Printer Name: HPLJ4

   In the lines provided, describe how to connect to Jacob HP Laser Jet 4 and print a document.

   _____

   _____

   _____

   _____

   _____

6. Alice has an HP LaserJet 6L at her desk. She telephones you because it won't print. She says that there is a yellow light flashing on the front panel and it is just sitting there. List at least three things you have Alice check to resolve her printing problem.

   _____

   _____

   _____

   _____

   _____

17

VIRUSES, DISASTER RECOVERY, AND A MAINTENANCE PLAN THAT WORKS

LABS INCLUDED IN THIS CHAPTER

♦ LAB 18.1 VIRUS PROTECTION

♦ LAB 18.2 CREATING AND MAINTAINING BACKUPS

♦ LAB 18.3 DESIGNING A PREVENTIVE MAINTENANCE PLAN

LAB 18.1 VIRUS PROTECTION

Objective

The objective of this lab exercise is to identify virus symptoms and learn how to use antivirus software to detect and disinfect viruses. After completing this lab exercise, you will be able to:

- Scan for viruses using antivirus software.
- Name some of the most common types of viruses.
- Describe the effects of several types of viruses.

Materials Required

This lab exercise requires one complete lab workstation for every two students. The lab workstation should meet the following requirements:

- 486 or better
- 16MB of RAM
- Windows 9x
- Nuts & Bolts software
- Access to the Internet

Lab Setup & Safety Tips

- Each lab workstation should have Windows 9x installed and functioning properly.
- Each lab workstation should have the Cheyenne Antivirus software installed prior to beginning the activities.

ACTIVITY

Scanning for viruses

1. Power on your lab workstation and allow it to boot into Windows 9x.
2. Click the **Start** button.
3. Point to **Programs**, and then point to **Nuts & Bolts**.
4. Click **Cheyenne Antivirus Scanner**.
5. In the Scanning box, type **c:**.
6. Click **Advanced**.
7. Verify that both the Boot Sector and the Files options are selected.
8. Click the **File Types** tab.
9. Verify that the **All Files** option is selected.
10. Click the **OK** button.
11. Click the **Start** button.

Researching viruses and describing their symptoms

1. In the following section you will research viruses and their symptoms. In each of the following categories, list five different types of viruses and describe their symptoms. Use the Internet as a research tool.

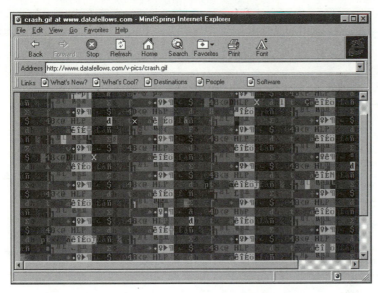

Figure 18-1   Crash virus (screen displays garbage, but no damage is done to the hard drive data)

a. Boot sector viruses

_____

_____

_____

_____

b. Worm

_____

_____

_____

_____

c. Trojan horse

_____

_____

_____

_____

18

d. Macro viruses

_____

_____

_____

_____

_____

e. Multipartite viruses

_____

_____

_____

_____

_____

f. Stealth viruses

_____

_____

_____

_____

_____

g. Partition table viruses

_____

_____

_____

_____

_____

h. Virus hoaxes

_____

_____

_____

_____

_____

Lab Notes

Where do viruses come from?—All viruses are written by programmers. You can contract a virus through many different forms of communication, such as disks, file downloads, and even Web sites.

A^+ **CERTIFICATION OBJECTIVES**

Table 18-1 DOS/Windows A+ Objectives

Objectives	Chapters	Page Numbers
4.4 Identify concepts relating to viruses and virus types—their danger, their symptoms, sources of viruses, how they infect, how to protect against them, and how to identify and remove them.	18	
A. What they are	18	982-993
B. Sources	18	982-993
C. How to determine presence	18	982-993

Review Questions

Circle True or False.

1. All viruses can cause fatal damage to your operating system. True / False

2. If your PC freezes often, you probably have a virus. True / False

3. Some viruses are designed to infect specific types of files such as Word 97 or Excel 97 documents. True / False

4. Currently there are 500 viruses in existence. True / False

5. Name three common ways viruses are contracted.

_____

_____

_____

_____

6. List two things you can do to help prevent the spread of viruses.

_____

_____

_____

_____

18

LAB 18.2 CREATING AND MAINTAINING BACKUPS

Objective

The objective of this lab exercise is to provide the hands-on experience necessary to properly install, configure, and execute a full backup in the Windows NT environment. After completing this lab exercise, you will be able to:

- Install an external tape backup device.
- Configure Windows NT workstation to use an external tape backup device.
- Use the Windows NT backup program.

Materials Required

This lab exercise requires one complete lab workstation for every four students. The lab workstations should meet the following requirements:

- 486 or better
- 16MB of RAM
- Windows NT

One external tape backup drive

One tape for the backup drive

Lab Setup & Safety Tips

- Each lab workstation should have Windows NT installed and functioning properly.
- Each lab workstation should have one network interface card installed.
- Students must follow standard ESD procedures when handling hardware.
- Always unplug the system unit before touching any component inside the case.
- Students should have the documentation and drivers necessary to install and configure the tape backup drive.

ACTIVITY

Installing a tape backup drive

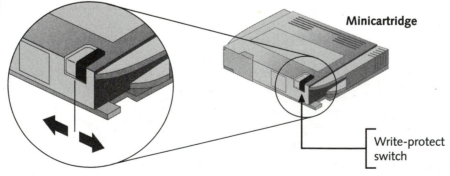

Figure 18-2   Minicartridge for a tape drive with write-protect switch

1. Power off your lab workstation.

2. Plug the parallel cable into the back of the tape drive.

3. Attach the parallel cable to the LPT1.

4. Plug in and power on the tape drive.

5. Power on your lab workstation and allow it to boot into Windows NT.

Installing the tape backup drive's device drivers

1. Click the **Start** button.

2. Point to **Settings** and click **Control Panel**.

3. Double-click the **Tape Devices** icon.

4. Click the **Drivers** tab.

5. Click the **Add** button.

6. Insert the disk containing the tape drive device drivers.

7. Click the **Have Disk** button.

8. Click the **OK** button.

9. Select the correct drivers for your tape drive.

10. Click the **OK** button.

11. If prompted, enter the path to the Windows NT installation files.

12. Click the **Close** button.

13. Click the **Yes** button to restart your computer.

Using the Windows NT backup program

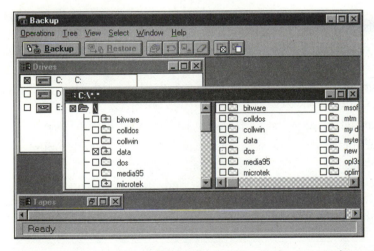

Figure 18-3 Windows NT backup utility similar to Windows 95 backup

1. Insert a tape into the tape backup drive.

2. Click the **Start** button.

3. Point to **Programs** and then click **Administrative Tools**.

4. Click the **Backup** option.

5. In the Backup program window, click the **Operations** menu.

6. Select the **Hardware Setup** option.

7. Verify that the proper tape backup device is shown in the Hardware Setup box.

8. Click the **OK** button.

9. Click the check box next to the C: drive to check it.

10. Click the **Operations** menu.

11. Click **Backup**.

Lab Notes

What is a differential backup?—A differential backup only backs up files that have changed or have been created since the last full backup.

What is an incremental backup?—An incremental backup only backs up files that have been changed or files that have been created since the last incremental or full backup.

CERTIFICATION OBJECTIVES

Table 18-2   DOS/Windows A+ Objectives

Objectives	Chapters	Page Numbers
1.4 Identify the procedures for basic disk management.	5, 6, 7, 18, Appendix F	
A. Using disk management utilities	6	320-322
B. Backing up	18	993, 999
C. Formatting	5, 6, 7	246, 283, 294, 361

Review Questions

Circle True or False.

1. The Windows NT Backup program allows you to back up files to either a floppy drive or a tape drive. True / False

2. You can install a tape drive device driver by using the Control Panel Add New Hardware icon. True / False

3. To begin a backup using the Windows NT Backup program, launch the Backup program, click the Tools menu, and then click Backup Now. True / False

4. Windows NT supports full, incremental, and differential backups. True / False

5. The Windows NT Backup program automatically backs up the PC nightly unless otherwise specified. True / False

6. Joy has decided to back up her hard drive. She understands how to execute the back-up process but is unsure what kind of backup she should perform (incremental, differential, or full). Explain below which type of backup Joy must use and why.

_____

_____

_____

_____

_____

LAB 18.3 DESIGNING A PREVENTIVE MAINTENANCE PLAN

Objective

The objective of this lab exercise is to create a preventive maintenance plan for a small business net-work. After completing this lab exercise, you will be able to:

- Design a preventive maintenance plan.

- Name some common preventive maintenance tasks for networked computers.

- Understand and describe the importance of maintenance delegation.

Materials Required

You will not require any additional materials for this exercise.

Lab Setup & Safety Tips

- Your instructor will discuss some common preventive maintenance procedures.

ACTIVITY

Developing a PC preventive maintenance plan

Table 18-3   Guidelines for developing a PC preventive maintenance plan

Component	Maintenance	How Often
Inside the case	■ Make sure air vents are clear. ■ Use compressed air to blow the dust out of the case. ■ Ensure that chips and expansion cards are firmly seated. ■ Clean the contacts on expansion cards.	Yearly
CMOS setup	■ Keep a backup record of setup (for example, use Nuts & Bolts rescue disk).	Whenever changes are made
Floppy drive	■ Only clean the floppy drive head when the drive does not work.	When the drive fails
Hard drive	■ Perform regular backups. ■ Automatically execute a virus scan program at startup. ■ Defragment the drive and recover lost clusters regularly. ■ Don't allow smoking around the PC. ■ Place the PC where it will not get kicked or bumped.	At least weekly At least daily Monthly
Keyboard	■ Keep the keyboard clean. ■ Keep the keyboard away from liquids.	Monthly Always
Mouse	■ Clean the mouse rollers and ball (see Chapter 7).	Monthly
Monitor	■ Clean the screen with a soft cloth.	At least monthly
Printers	■ Clean out the dust and bits of paper. ■ Clean the paper and ribbon paths with a soft cloth. ■ Don't re-ink ribbons or use recharged toner cartridges.	At least monthly

18

Table 18-3   Guidelines for developing a PC preventive maintenance plan (continued)

Component	Maintenance	How Often
Software	▪ If so directed by your employer, check that only authorized software is present. ▪ Regularly remove files from the Recycle Bin and \Temp directories. ▪ Remove any temporary files in the /DOS directory.	At least monthly
Written record	▪ Record all software, including version numbers and the OS installed on the PC. ▪ Record all hardware components installed, including hardware settings. ▪ Record when and what preventive maintenance is performed. ▪ Record any repairs done to the PC.	Whenever changes are made

1. You are the network administrator for a 75-user network. Your employer has asked you to create a preventive maintenance plan for all of the hardware components connected to the network. You have started this project by creating the following list, which contains each of the hardware components that should be included in the preventive maintenance plan. Using the table above for reference, write at least two preventive maintenance tasks for each of the listed hardware components. Be sure to state how often the preventive maintenance task should be completed and who should be responsible for completing the tasks (that is, yourself or the user). Remember that you are the only network administrator and will not realistically be able to complete every preventive maintenance task necessary to maintain a network of this size.

   a. **System unit**

      i. PM Task 1

      _____

      _____

      _____

      ii. PM Task 2

      _____

      _____

      _____

   b. **CMOS setup**

      i. PM Task 1

      _____

      _____

      _____

ii. PM Task 2

_____

_____

_____

c. **Floppy drive**

   i. PM Task 1

_____

_____

_____

  ii. PM Task 2

_____

_____

_____

d. **Hard drive**

   i. PM Task 1

_____

_____

  ii. PM Task 2

_____

_____

_____

e. **Keyboard and mouse**

   i. PM Task 1

_____

_____

  ii. PM Task 2

_____

_____

_____

f. **Monitors**

   i. PM Task 1

_____

_____

_____

18

ii. PM Task 2

_____

_____

_____

g. **10 Laser printers**

i. PM Task 1

_____

_____

_____

ii. PM Task 2

_____

_____

_____

h. **7 Inkjet printers**

i. PM Task 1

_____

_____

_____

ii. PM Task 2

_____

_____

_____

Lab Notes

What is a PM kit?—PM kits, or preventive maintenance kits, are designed to keep printers in good working order. A PM kit normally is administered during off-business hours to refresh and revitalize printer components that receive the most wear.

A+ CERTIFICATION OBJECTIVES

Table 18-4 Core A+ Objectives

Objectives	Chapters	Page Numbers
3.1 Identify the purpose of various types of preventive maintenance products and procedures and when to use/perform them.	17, 18	
A. Liquid cleaning compounds	18	978, 979
B. Types of materials to clean contacts and connections	17, 18	941, 978, 979
C. Vacuum out systems, power supplies, fans	18	978, 979

Review Questions

Circle True or False.

1. Tasks in a preventive maintenance plan must be completed only by the network administrator. True / False

2. PM kits are designed to minimize printer downtime. True / False

3. Shaking the dust out of a system unit is considered an excellent preventive maintenance task that should be completed once a month. True / False

4. Smoking around a hard drive can shorten its life. True / False

5. If all of the client computers are using the Windows NT operating system, you will not need to create a preventive maintenance program. True / False

18

19

THE PROFESSIONAL PC TECHNICIAN

LABS INCLUDED IN THIS CHAPTER

♦ **LAB 19.1** TELEPHONE SUPPORT

♦ **LAB 19.2** ON-SITE SUPPORT

♦ **LAB 19.3** DOCUMENTING YOUR WORK

LAB 19.1 TELEPHONE SUPPORT

Objective

The objective of this lab exercise is to simulate a technical support call. After completing this lab exercise, you will be able to:

- Troubleshoot both hardware and software problems over the phone.
- Describe the advantages and disadvantages of supporting PCs over the phone.
- Understand the importance of listening to your customer.

Materials Required

This lab exercise requires one complete lab workstation for every two students. The lab workstations should meet the following requirements:

- 486 or better
- 16MB of RAM
- Windows 9x
- One modem

Lab Setup & Safety Tips

- The modem should be installed and functioning properly prior to beginning the activity.
- During this lab exercise you will be simulating a telephone support call. For the most realistic results, the student in the role of the technician should not be able to see what his or her customer is doing on the lab workstation.
- If students are working in pairs, designate one as Student 1 and one as Student 2.

ACTIVITY

Student 2 (Customer)

In this activity, you will delete the currently installed modem. After restarting your computer, you then will call your customer support line.

1. Power on your lab workstation and allow it to boot into Windows 9x.
2. Right-click the **My Computer** icon.
3. Select **Properties** from the shortcut menu.
4. Click the **Device Manager** tab.
5. Click **Modem**.
6. Select the installed modem, press the **Delete** key, and then click the **OK** button.
7. Click the **Close** button.
8. Click the **Yes** button when prompted to restart your computer.
9. Call the customer support line, and explain that you have installed a modem but can't get it to dial.

Student 1 (Technician)

The only resources you should have during this simulation are a pen and a piece of paper. After providing telephone support to your customer, answer the following questions.

Were there any error messages? If so, write them down:

_____

_____

_____

What was the problem?

_____

_____

_____

List several (at least three) clues that helped lead you to the problem (include the customer dialog):

_____

_____

_____

What would you do differently in the future to improve your troubleshooting process?

_____

_____

_____

Student 1 (Customer)

You are calling customer support (Student 2) because you recently purchased some memory, but you are not sure how to install it.

1. Power off your lab workstation and unplug it.

2. Remove the case.

3. Remove all of the RAM.

4. Call the customer support line, explain that you have removed the case, and you now want to install your new memory (use the memory you removed as the new memory).

Student 2 (Technician)

The only resources you should have during this simulation are a pen and a piece of paper. After providing telephone support to your customer, answer the following questions:

Were there any error messages? If so, write them down:

_____

_____

_____

What was the problem?

_____

_____

_____

List several (at least three) clues that helped lead you to the problem (include the customer dialog):

_____

_____

_____

19

What would you do differently in the future to improve your troubleshooting process?

_____

_____

_____

Lab Notes

Listening to your customers—While working through this lab exercise, you probably discovered the importance of listening to your customer. At the beginning of a support call it is a good idea to allow your customer to describe the problem in detail and explain each step he or she has taken prior to the call. A good technician listens to the customer and at times even allows the customer to troubleshoot the problem. Some customers already know the answer to their problem, but lack the confidence to follow through.

Maintaining control of a call—Although it is important to listen to your customers, don't lose control of the conversation or situation. If you feel you are losing control, ask your customer any questions you need answered and then reiterate what they say to you. At this point explain to the customer the next step to resolving their problem, and make sure that this is acceptable.

A+ CERTIFICATION OBJECTIVES

Table 19-1   Core A+ Objectives

Objectives	Chapters	Page Numbers
2.2 Identify basic troubleshooting procedures and good practices for eliciting problem symptoms from customers.	8, Appendix A	
A. Troubleshooting/isolation/problem determination procedures.	8	416-420
B. Determine whether hardware or software problem.	8	416-420
C. Gather information from user regarding, e.g., multimeter.	8	416-420
D. Customer Environment	8	416-420
E. Symptoms/Error Codes	8, Appendix A	416-420, A1, A2
F. Situation when the problem occurred	8	416-421
8.1 Differentiate effective from ineffective behaviors as these contribute to the maintenance or achievement of customer satisfaction.	19	1019-1028
A. Communicating and listening (face-to-face or over the phone)	19	1019-1028
B. Interpreting verbal and nonverbal cues	19	1019-1028
C. Responding appropriately to the customer's technical level	19	1019-1028
D. Establishing personal rapport with the customer	19	1019-1028
E. Professional conduct, for example, punctuality, accountability	19	1019-1028
F. Helping and guiding a customer with problem descriptions	19	1019-1028

Table 19-1 Core A+ Objectives (continued)

Objectives	Chapters	Page Numbers
G. Responding to and closing a service call	19	1019-1028
H. Handling complaints and upset customers, conflict avoidance, and resolution	19	1019-1028
I. Showing empathy and flexibility	19	1019-1028
J. Sharing the customer's sense of urgency	19	1019-1028

Review Questions

Circle True or False.

1. As a technician you should always be sensitive to your customer's situation. True / False

2. Always tell your customers what to do. True / False

3. Customers often can provide clues to their problem. True / False

4. What do you think are the three most important personality traits a help desk technician should have?

_____

_____

_____

LAB 19.2 ON-SITE SUPPORT

Objective

The objective of this lab exercise is to simulate a desktop PC support call. After completing this lab exercise you will be able to:

- Troubleshoot both hardware and software problems while communicating with a customer.

- Describe the advantages and disadvantages of desktop support.

Materials Required

This lab exercise requires one complete lab workstation for every two students. The lab workstation should meet the following requirements:

- 486 or better

- 16MB of RAM

- Windows 9x

One DOS system disk

Lab Setup & Safety Tips

- Each lab workstation should have Windows 9x installed and functioning properly.

- If students are working in pairs, designate one as Student 1 and one as Student 2.

19

ACTIVITY

Student 2 (Customer)

You have called a technician out to your desk because your system won't boot and is giving you the error message "Invalid or missing command interpreter: command.com". Complete the following steps while Student 1 is away from the lab workstation.

1. Insert a system disk in drive A.

2. Power on your lab workstation and allow it to boot from the system disk.

3. At the A prompt, type **C:** and press **Enter**.

4. Type **REN C:\COMMAND.COM C:\COMMAND.OLD**.

5. Press **Enter**.

6. Type **REN C:\MSDOS.SYS C:\MSDOS.OLD**.

7. Press **Enter**.

8. Reboot your lab workstation and verify that you receive the error message, "Invalid or missing command interpreter: command.com".

9. Ask your technical support person for help. Explain that you just installed some registry cleaning software and now nothing works right.

Student 1 (Technician)

The only resources you should have during this simulation are a pen and a piece of paper. After providing on-site support, answer the following questions:

Were there any error messages? If so, write them down:

_____

_____

_____

What was the problem?

_____

_____

_____

List several (at least three) clues that helped lead you to the problem (include the customer dialog):

_____

_____

_____

What would you do differently in the future to improve your troubleshooting process?

_____

_____

_____

Student 1 (Customer)

You will reposition the RAM so your system won't boot. Complete the following steps while Student 2 is away from the lab workstation.

1. Power off and unplug the lab workstation.
2. Remove the case.
3. Unplug the data cable to the hard drive.
4. Change the jumper to the slave position.
5. Reposition the RAM and move it into the wrong banks.
6. Replace the case.
7. Power on the lab workstation and enter the Setup program.
8. Remove the hard drive from the Setup program.
9. Save the changes and exit.
10. Ask your technical support person for help. Explain that you didn't touch anything except the memory because you just installed new memory.

Student 2 (Technician)

The only resources you should have during this simulation are a pen and a piece of paper. After providing on-site support, answer the following questions:

Were there any error messages? If so, write them down:

_____

_____

_____

What was the problem?

_____

_____

_____

List several (at least three) clues that helped lead you to the problem (include the customer dialog):

_____

_____

_____

What would you do differently in the future to improve your troubleshooting process?

_____

_____

_____

 Lab Notes

Safe Mode—Safe Mode is a Windows 9x troubleshooting mode. When Windows 9x is started in Safe Mode, it will load only a minimal set of drivers that are necessary to load Windows. You can boot Windows 9x into Safe Mode by pressing the F8 key during the boot process.

19

A^+ CERTIFICATION OBJECTIVES

Table 19-2   Core A+ Objectives

Objectives	Chapters	Page Numbers
2.2 Identify basic troubleshooting procedures and good practices for eliciting problem symptoms from customers.	8, Appendix A	
A. Troubleshooting/isolation/problem determination procedures.	8	416-420
B. Determine whether hardware or software problem.	8	416-420
C. Gather information from user regarding, e.g., multimeter.	8	416-420
D. Customer Environment	8	416-420
E. Symptoms/Error Codes	8, Appendix A	416-420, A1, A2
F. Situation when the problem occurred	8	416, 421
8.1 Differentiate effective from ineffective behaviors as these contribute to the maintenance or achievement of customer satisfaction.	19	
A. Communicating and listening (face-to-face or over the phone)	19	1019-1028
B. Interpreting verbal and nonverbal cues	19	1019-1028
C. Responding appropriately to the customer's technical level	19	1019-1028
D. Establishing personal rapport with the customer	19	1019-1028
E. Professional conduct, for example, punctuality, accountability	19	1019-1028
F. Helping and guiding a customer with problem descriptions	19	1019-1028
G. Responding to and closing a service call	19	1019-1028
H. Handling complaints and upset customers, conflict avoidance, and resolution	19	1019-1028
I. Showing empathy and flexibility	19	1019-1028
J. Sharing the customer's sense of urgency	19	1019-1028

Table 19-3   DOS/Windows A+ Objectives

Objectives	Chapters	Page Numbers
4.1 Recognize and interpret the meaning of common error codes and startup messages from the boot sequence, and identify steps to correct the problems.	4, 5, 7, 8, 12, Appendices A and E	
A. Safe Mode	8, Appendix E	427, 428, E5
C. No operating system found	8, Appendix A	425, 426, A2
F. Himem.sys not loaded	4	198, 199
G. Missing or corrupt Himem.sys	4	198, 199
4.2 Recognize Windows-specific printing problems and identify the procedures for correcting them.	17	

Review Questions

Circle True or False.

1. You can use Safe Mode to troubleshoot Windows 9x. True / False

2. You can enter Safe Mode by pressing the F8 key during the boot process. True / False

3. Windows 9x doesn't need the COMMAND.COM or MSDOS.SYS files. True / False

4. Troubleshooting the Windows NT environment is similar to troubleshooting the Windows 9x environment. True / False

5. Describe how a Windows 9x repair disk can be used to repair the Windows 9x startup environment.

6. Lesa has decided to clean some files off her hard drive but isn't sure which files are safe to delete. Make Lesa a list of five files that she should not delete.

_____

_____

_____

LAB 19.3 DOCUMENTING YOUR WORK

Objective

The objective of this lab exercise is to document your work from the previous lab exercises. After completing this lab exercise, you will be able to:

- Complete a standard service-call report form.
- Complete a standard help desk call report form.
- Describe the values of A+ certification.

Materials Required

You will not require any additional materials for this lab exercise.

Lab Setup & Safety Tips

- To complete the following activity you must have already completed Labs 19.1 and 19.2.

19

ACTIVITY

Documenting Your Help Desk Call (from Lab 19.1)

1. Complete the following Help Desk Report Form with the information from the activities in Lab 19.1.

Help Desk Call Report Form

Call

Caller:_____   Date:_____ Time:_____
Location:_____   Phone:_____
Received by:_____
Description:_____
_____

Notes on the Call

_____
_____
_____
_____

Follow-up Call on _____ By _____

_____
_____

Follow-up Call on _____ By _____

_____
_____

Outcome of Call

_____ ☐ Solved
_____ ☐ Unresolved
_____
_____

Figure 19-1   Help Desk Call Report Form

Documenting Your PC Support Call (from Lab 19.2)

1. Complete the following Service Call Report Form with the information from the activities in Lab 19.2.

Service Call Report Form

Initial Request

Requested by:_____ Date:_____Time:_____
Received by:_____ Phone 1:_____
                                Phone 2:_____
Description of problem:_____
_____

Initial Action

Advice: _____
Appointment Made:
        By: _____ Date:_____Time:_____
        Directions:_____

Source of Problem

_____ ☐ Hardware
_____ ☐ Software
_____ ☐ User
_____

Solution or Outcome

_____ ☐ Repair
_____ ☐ Replace
_____ ☐ Educate
_____ ☐ Other

Notes

_____
_____
_____

Figure 19-2   Service Call Report Form

Lab Notes

What are the advantages of A+ certification?—A+ certification is an industry-recognized proof of competence and will greatly improve/increase your job opportunities.

What are your copyright responsibilities?—You are responsible for complying with the license agreement of the software package you are installing. It is also your responsibility to purchase only legitimate software packages that are properly licensed. You should report any software piracy issue by calling 1-888-NOPIRACY.

19

Other Technical Support Resources

Table 19-4   Technical support Web sites

Web Site	Responsible Organization
www.aserve.net	Advanced Services Network
www.byte.com	BYTE Magazine
www.cnet.com	CNET, Inc.
www.cybercollege.com	CyberCollege
www.datafellows.com	Data Fellows Inc.
www.modems.com	Zoom Telephonics, Inc.
www.pc-today.com	PC Today Online
www.pcwebopedia.com	internet.com Corporation
www.pcworld.com	PC World
www.sangoma.com	Sangoma Technologies, Inc.
www.Tomshardware.com	Tom's Hardware Guide
www.tcp.ca	The Computer Paper
www.winfiles.com	Steve Jenkins and Jenesys, LLC.
www.zdnet.com	ZDNet (Publishes several technical magazines)

A+ CERTIFICATION OBJECTIVES

Table 19-5   Core A+ Objectives

Objectives	Chapters	Page Numbers
8.1 Differentiate effective from ineffective behaviors as these contribute to the maintenance or achievement of customer satisfaction.	19	1027-1028

Review Questions

Circle True or False.

1. Copyright protection is everyone's responsibility. True / False

2. One of your customers, John, asked you several weeks ago to create a shortcut to File Manager for him. He has now called you back in frustration because the shortcut you made has stopped working. Describe the best way to diffuse this situation.

   _____

   _____

   _____

3. List at least three reasons why call report forms are used.

   _____

   _____

4. Cindy has no previous experience working on a PC. To complete her job duties, she must be able to use Microsoft Word. List five or more things you would teach Cindy to help her get started successfully.

   _____

   _____

   _____